P9-DJA-098

When in French

When in French

LOVE IN A SECOND LANGUAGE

Lauren Collins

PENGUIN PRESS
NEW YORK
2016

PENGUIN PRESS
An imprint of Penguin Random House LLC
375 Hudson Street
New York, New York 10014
penguin.com

Copyright © 2016 by Lauren Collins
Penguin supports copyright. Copyright fuels creativity, encourages diverse voices, promotes free speech, and creates a vibrant culture. Thank you for buying an authorized edition of this book and for complying with copyright laws by not reproducing, scanning, or distributing any part of it in any form without permission. You are supporting writers and allowing Penguin to continue to publish books for every reader.

Excerpt from "For Me . . . For-mi-da-ble," original French text by Jacques Plante, music by Charles Aznavour. © Copyright 1963 (renewed) Editions Musicales Charles Aznavour, Paris, France. TRO-Hampshire House Publishing Corp., New York, controls all publication rights for the United States and Canada.

LIBRARY OF CONGRESS CATALOGING-IN-PUBLICATION DATA
Names: Collins, Lauren (Journalist)
Title: When in French : love in a second language / Lauren Collins.
Description: New York : Penguin Press, 2016.
Identifiers: LCCN 2016017611 | ISBN 9781594206443 (hardback) | ISBN 9780698191075 (e-book)
Subjects: LCSH: Collins, Lauren (Journalist) | Journalists—United States—Biography. | Travelers' writings, American—France. | French language—Conversations and phrases—English. | French language—Self-instruction. | French language—Study and teaching—English speakers. | France—Languages. | BISAC: BIOGRAPHY & AUTOBIOGRAPHY / Literary. | TRAVEL / Europe / France. | HUMOR / Topic / Marriage & Family.
Classification: LCC PN4874.C646 A3 2016 | DDC 448.0092 [B]—dc23 LC record available at https://lccn.loc.gov/2016017611

Printed in the United States of America
1 3 5 7 9 10 8 6 4 2

Designed by Amanda Dewey

Penguin is committed to publishing works of quality and integrity. In that spirit, we are proud to offer this book to our readers; however, the story, the experiences, and the words are the author's alone.

For Olivier

You are the one for me, for me, for me, *formidable*

But how can you

See me, see me, see me, *si minable*

Je ferais mieux d'aller choisir mon vocabulaire

Pour te plaire

Dans la langue de Molière

—Charles Aznavour, "For Me, *For-mi-da-ble*"

Contents

When in French

One

THE PAST PERFECT

Le Plus-que-parfait

I HADN'T WANTED to live in Geneva. In fact, I had decisively wished not to, but there I was. Plastic ficuses flanked the entryway of the building. The corrugated brown carpet matched the matte brown fretwork of the elevator cage. The ground floor hosted the offices of a psychiatrist and those of an *iridologue*—a practitioner of a branch of alternative medicine that was popularized when, in 1861, a Hungarian physician noticed similar streaks of color in the eyeballs of a broken-legged man and a broken-legged owl. Our apartment was one story up.

The bell rang. Newlywed and nearly speechless, I cracked open the door, a slab of oak with a beveled brass knob. Next to it, the landlord had installed a nameplate, giving the place the look less of a home than of a bilingual tax firm.

A man stood on the landing. He was dressed in black—T-shirt, pants, tool belt. A length of cord coiled around his left shoulder. In his right hand, he held a brush. Creosote darkened his face and arms, extending his sleeves to his fingernails and the underside of his palms. A red bandanna was tied around his neck. He actually wore a top hat. I hesitated before pushing the door open further, unsure whether I was up against a chimney sweep or some sort of Swiss strip-o-gram.

"Bonjour," I said, exhausting approximately half of my French vocabulary.

The man, remaining clothed, returned my greeting and began to explain why he was there. His words, though I couldn't understand them, jogged secondhand snatches of dialogue: per cantonal law, as the landlord had explained to my husband, who had transmitted the command to me, we had to have our fireplace cleaned once a year.

I led the chimney sweep to the living room. It was dominated by the fireplace, an antique thing in dark striated marble, with pot hooks and a pair of side ducts whose covers hinged open like lockets. Shifting his weight onto one leg with surprising grace, the chimney sweep leaned forward and stuck his head under the mantel. He poked around for a few minutes, letting out the occasional wheeze. Coming out of the arabesque, he turned to me and began, again, to speak.

On a musical level, whatever he was saying sounded cheerful, a scale-skittering ditty of *le*s and *la*s. Perhaps he was admiring the condition of the damper, or welcoming me to the neighborhood. He reached into his pocket, proffering a matchbook and a disc of cork. Then he disappeared.

Minutes went by as I examined his gifts. They seemed like props for a magic trick. More minutes passed. I launched into a version of rock, scissors, paper: since the cork couldn't conceivably do anything to the matches, then the matches must be meant to light the cork. Action was required, but I feared potentially incinerating the chimney sweep, who, I guessed, was making some sort of inspection up on the roof.

Eventually he returned, chirping out some more instructions. I performed a repertoire of reassuring eyebrow raises and comprehending head nods. He scampered away. I still had no idea, so I lit a match, held it to the cork, and tossed it behind the grate. The pile started smoking and hissing. After a few seconds, I lost my nerve and snuffed it out.

The chimney sweep resurfaced, less jolly. He had appointed an assistant who, it appeared, was actively thwarting his routine. This time he spoke in the supple, obvious tones one reserves for madwomen, especially those in possession of flammable objects. Reclaiming the half-charred piece of cork, he lit a fire and, potbelly jiggling, sprinted back out the door.

Finally, he returned and reported—I assume, since we used the fireplace without incident all that winter—that everything was in order.

"Au revoir!" I said, trying to regain his confidence, and my standing as chatelaine of this strange, drab domain. "Hello" and "good-bye" were a pair of bookends, propping up a vast library of blank volumes, void almanacs, novels full of sentiment I couldn't apprehend. It felt as though the instruction manual to living in Switzerland had been written in invisible ink.

I HAD MOVED to Geneva a month earlier to be with my husband, Olivier, who had moved there because his job required him to. My restaurant French was just passable. Drugstore French was a stretch. IKEA French was pretty much out of the question, meaning that, since Olivier, a native speaker, worked twice as many hours a week as Swiss stores were open, we went for months without things like lamps.

He had already been living in Geneva for a year and a half. Meanwhile, I had remained in London, where we'd met. The commute was tolerable, then tiring. In the spring of 2013, as our wedding approached, it was becoming a drag. Finally, that June, a visa fiasco abruptly forced me to leave England. Memoirs of immigration, like memories of immigration, often begin with a sense of approach—the ship sailing into the harbor, the blurred countryside through the windows of a train. My arrival in Geneva, on British Airways, was a perfect anticlimax, the modern ache of displacement anesthetized amid blank corridors of orange liqueur and fountain pens.

When Lord Byron arrived in Switzerland for an extended holiday in May 1816—fleeing creditors, gossips, and his wife, from whom he had recently separated, after likely fathering a child with his half sister—his entourage included a valet, a footman, a personal physician, a monkey, and a peacock. That summer he wrote *The Prisoner of Chillon*, the tale of a sixteenth-century Genevan monk, most of whose family has been killed in battle or burned at the stake. "There were no stars, no earth, no time / No check, no change, no good, no crime," the poem reads. As a description of the local atmosphere, that seemed to me about right. Geneva was unlovely, but not hideous, as though no one had cared enough to do ugly with conviction. The city seemed suffused by complacency, as gray and costive as the clouds that hovered over Lac Léman.

The main attraction was a clock made of begonias. Transportation was by tram. At the Office Cantonal de la Population, I was given a "Practical Guide to Living in Geneva," ostensibly a welcome booklet. "It is forbidden and not well looked upon to make too much noise in your apartment between 21:00 and 07:00," it read. "Also avoid talking too loudly, and shouting to call someone in public places." The booklet directed me to a web page, which listed further gradations of *bruit admissible* (acceptable noise) and *bruit excessif* (excessive noise). Vacuuming during the day was okay, but God help the voluptuary who ran the washing machine after work.

Geneva had long been a place of asylum, but its tradition of liberty in the religious and political realms had never given rise to a libertine scene. Even though nearly half of the population was foreign-born, the city remained resolutely uncosmopolitan, a tepid fondue of tearooms, confectionaries, and storefronts selling things like hosiery and lutes. Every block had its *coiffeur*, just as every *coiffeur* had its lone patroness, getting her hair washed in the sink. It wasn't as though Genevans enjoyed the advantages of living in the countryside. Many of them, native and nouveau, had means. So why hadn't some son or daughter of the city, after traveling to New York or Paris or Beirut—to Dallas or Manchester—been inspired to open a place where the bread didn't come in a doily-lined wicker basket? Was there a dinkier phrase, in any language, than *métropole lémanique*?

After a month or so of heavy tramming, we decided to buy a car. We purchased insurance, which included coverage for theft, fire, natural disasters, and *dommages causés par les fouines*—damages caused by a type of local weasel. I traded in my American driver's license for a Swiss one. The process took seventeen minutes flat. One sodden afternoon not long after, we trammed over to the Citroën lot.

Alexandre, a customer service representative, greeted us. He smelled of cigarettes and was wearing a tie.

"So, *voici*," he said. (Switzerland has four official languages—German, French, Italian, and Romansh—and people tended to switch back and forth without warning, with varying degrees of success.) He led us to the car, a used hatchback parked outside the office on a covered ramp.

It was pouring, each drop of rain a suicide jumper, hurling itself onto the ramp's tin roof. We circled the car, hoping to project a discerning vibe, as though any painted-over weasel damage would never get by us.

Olivier stopped on the car's left side and, because it seemed like the thing to do, opened the backseat door.

"You will soon have *des petits enfants*?" Alexandre said.

"Um, we just got married."

"*Ah, bon?* It was a Protestant or a Catholic ceremony?"

Our city hall wedding was an unimaginability for Alexandre. I was beginning to understand, only very slowly, that the city's conservatism was neither an accident of demographics nor an oversight but an enactment of its founding values by conscious design. In 1387, more than a hundred years before the Catholic Church began to loosen its prohibitions on usury, the bishop of Geneva signed a charter of liberties, granting the *genevois*, alone in Christendom, the privilege of lending money at interest. The elite became financiers. The aspirant became Swiss mercenaries. Famed for their ferocity with the halberd and the pike, they poured cash into the economy in an era when most of the world's population was getting paid in eggs.

The mentality had persisted: do your hell-raising—your eating in restaurants without doilies—abroad, and retreat to a place of imperturbable security. Voltaire wrote of Geneva, "There, one calculates, and never laughs." Stendhal, passing through seventy years later, concluded that the *genevois*, despite their wealth and worldly networks, were at heart a parochial people: "Their sweetest pleasure, when they are young, is to dream that one day they will be rich. Even when they indulge in some imprudence and abandon themselves to pleasure, the ones they choose are rustic and cheap: a walk, to the summit of some mountain where they drink milk." Monotony, then, was an economy. So that we could collectively accrue more capital, a curfew had been set.

Weekends were the worst. All of the shops closed at seven—except on Thursdays, when some of them closed at seven thirty—rendering Saturdays a dull frenzy of provisioning. Sundays were desolate, a relic of the Calvinist lockdown mentality that had sent the young Rousseau scrambling to Savoy. A relocation consultant furnished by Olivier's company said that there had been talk of easing the Sunday moratorium, but to no avail. "Approximately ninety-nine percent of Swiss people support it," he said, sounding to us approximately one hundred percent like a Swiss person.

Geneva had its graces—the trams operated on an honor system; even the graffiti artists were mannerly, defacing the sides of statues that didn't face the street—but I took them as further proof that the city was second-rate. You could, of course, escape to any number of attractive places within driving range, and we passed many afternoons wandering the relatively bustling streets of Lyon. It seemed sad, though, that the main selling point of the place where we lived was its proximity to places where we'd rather live. And while the mountains that surrounded us were magnificent, the twenty-five or so times a year that we managed to take advantage of them didn't make up for the three hundred and forty times we didn't. On Sunday nights, after an outing, we'd return to our stockpiled supper and take out the recycling, casting bottles and cans into the maw of a public bin. This was our version of indulging in an imprudence: you could get fined for recycling—*for* recycling, I had not missed a negative adverb—on the day of rest.

Behind its orderly facade—the apartment buildings with

their sauerkraut paint jobs; the matrons in furs; the brutalist plazas; the allées of pollarded trees—Geneva was, if anything, faintly sinister. Its vaunted sense of discretion seemed a cover for dodginess, bourgeois respectability masking a sleazy milieu. What was going on in those clinics and *cabinets*? Whose money, obtained by what means, was stashed in the private banks? What was a "family office," anyway?

One day I received an e-mail from the Intercontinental Hotel Genève, entitled "What You Didn't Know about Geneva." I did not know that the Intercontinental Hotel Genève "continues to cater to the likes of the Saudi Royal family and the ruling family of the United Arab Emirates," that the most expensive bottle of wine sold at auction was sold in Geneva (1947 Château Cheval Blanc, $304,375), that the most expensive diamond in the world was sold in Geneva (the Pink Star, a 59.6-carat oval-cut pink diamond, $83 million), or that Geneva "has witnessed numerous world records, such as the world's longest candy cane, measuring 51 feet long." I developed a theory I thought of as the Édouard Stern principle, after the French investment banker who was found dead in a penthouse apartment in Geneva—shot four times, wearing a flesh-colored latex catsuit, trussed. Read any truly tawdry news story, and Geneva will somehow play into it by the fifth paragraph. Balzac wrote that behind every great fortune lies a crime. In Switzerland, behind every crime seemed to lie a great fortune.

Around us Europe was reeling, but the stability of the Swiss franc, combined with the influx of people who sought to exploit it, made the city profoundly expensive. The stores were full of things we neither wanted nor could afford. I reacted by refusing to buy or do anything that I thought cost too much money, which was pretty much everything, and then complaining about my boredom. Geneva syndrome: becoming as tedious as your captor. The expanses of my calendar stretched as pristine as those of the Alps.

Olivier didn't love Geneva either, but he didn't experience it as an effacement. He said that it reminded him of a provincial French town in the 1980s—a setting and an epoch with which he was well acquainted, having grown up an hour outside Bordeaux during the Mitterrand years. His consolations were familiarities: reciting the call-and-response of francophone pleasantries with the women at the dry cleaners; reading *Le Canard enchaîné*, the French satirical newspaper, when it came out each Wednesday; watching the TV shows—many of them seemed to involve puppets—that he knew from home. He was living in a sitcom, with a laugh track and wacky neighbors. I was stranded in a silent film.

WE HAD ESTABLISHED our life together, in London, on more or less neutral ground: his continent, my language. It worked. Olivier was my guide to living outside of the behemoth of American culture; I was his guide to living inside the behemoth of English.

He had learned the language over the course of many years. When he was sixteen, his parents sent him to Saugerties, New York, for six weeks: a homestay with some acquaintances of an English teacher in Bordeaux, the only American they knew. Olivier landed at JFK, where a taxi picked him up. This was around the time of the Atlanta Olympic Games.

"What is the English for 'female athlete'?" he asked, wanting to be able to discuss current events.

"'Bitch,'" the driver said.

They drove on toward Ulster County, Olivier straining for a glimpse of the famed Manhattan skyline. The patriarch of the host family was an arborist named Vern. Olivier remembers driving around Saugerties with Charlene, Vern's wife, and a friend of hers, who begged him over and over again to say "hamburger." He was mystified by the fact that Charlene called Vern "the Incredible Hunk."

Five years later Olivier found himself in England, a graduate student in mathematics. Unfortunately, his scholastic English—"Kevin is a blue-eyed boy" had been billed as a canonical phrase—had done little to prepare him for the realities of the language on the ground. "You've really improved," his roommate told him, six weeks into the term. "When you got here, you couldn't speak a word." At that point, Olivier had been studying English for more than a decade.

After England, he moved to California to study for a PhD, still barely able to cobble together a sentence. His debut as a teaching assistant for a freshman course in calculus was greeted by a mass defection. On the plus side, one day he looked out upon the residue of the crowd and noticed an attentive female student. She was wearing a T-shirt that read "Bonjour, Paris!"

By the time we met, Olivier had become not only a proficient English speaker but a sensitive, agile one. Upon arriving in London in 2007, he'd had to take an English test to obtain his license as an amateur pilot. The examiner rated him "Expert": "Able to speak at length with a natural, effortless flow. Varies speech flow for stylistic effect, e.g. to emphasize a point. Uses appropriate discourse markers and connectors spontaneously." He was funny, quick, and colloquial. He wrote things like (before our third date), "Trying to think of an alternative to the bar-restaurant diptych, but maybe that's too ambitious." He said things like (riffing on a line from *Zoolander* as he pulled the car up, once again, to the right-hand curb), "I'm not an ambi-parker." I rarely gave any thought to the fact that English wasn't his native tongue.

One day, at the movies, he approached the concession stand, taking out his wallet.

"A medium popcorn, a Sprite, and a Pepsi, please."

"Wait a second," I said. "Did you just specifically order a Pepsi?"

In a word, Olivier had been outed. Due to a traumatic experience at a drive-through in California, he confessed, he still didn't permit himself to pronounce the word "Coke" aloud. For me, it was a shocking discovery, akin to finding out that a peacock couldn't really fly. I felt extreme tenderness toward his vulnerability, mingled with wonderment at his ingenuity. I'd had no idea that he still, very occasionally, approached English in a defensive posture, feinting and dodging as he strutted along.

I only knew Olivier in his third language—he also spoke Spanish, the native language of his maternal grandparents, who had fled over the Pyrenees during the Spanish Civil War—but his powers of expression were one of the things that made me fall in love with him. For all his rationality, he had a romantic streak, an attunement to the currents of feeling that run beneath the surface of words. Once he wrote me a letter—an inducement to what we might someday have together—in which every sentence began with "Maybe." Maybe he'd make me an omelet, he said, every day of my life.

We moved in together before long. One night, we were watching a movie. I spilled a glass of water, and went to mop it up with some paper towels.

"They don't have very good capillarity," Olivier said.

"Huh?" I replied, continuing to dab at the puddle.

"Their capillarity isn't very good."

"What are you talking about? That's not even a word."

Olivier said nothing. A few days later, I noticed a piece of paper lying in the printer tray. It was a page from the Merriam-Webster online dictionary:

capillarity ***noun*** ka-pə-ˈler-ə-tē, -ˈla-rə-

1: the property or state of being capillary

2: the action by which the surface of a liquid where it is in contact with a solid (as in a capillary tube) is elevated or depressed depending on the relative attraction of the molecules of the liquid for each other and for those of the solid

Ink to a nib, my heart surged.

There was eloquence, too, in the way he expressed himself physically—a perfect grammar of balanced steps and filled glasses and fingertips on the back of my elbow, predicated on some quiet confidence that we were always already a compound subject. The first time we said good-bye, he put his hands around my waist and lifted me just half an inch off the ground: a kiss in commas. I was short; he was not much taller. We could look each other in the eye.

But despite the absence of any technical barrier to comprehension, we often had, in some weirdly basic sense, a hard time understanding each other. The critic George Steiner defined intimacy as "confident, quasi-immediate translation," a state of increasingly one-to-one correspondence in which "the external vulgate and the private mass of language grow more and more concordant." Translation, he explained, occurs both across and *inside* languages. You are performing a feat of interpretation anytime you attempt to communicate with someone who is not like you.

In addition to being French and American, Olivier and I were translating, to varying degrees, across a host of Steiner's categories: scientist/artist, atheist/believer, man/woman. It seemed sometimes as if generation was one of the few gaps across which we weren't attempting to stretch ourselves. I had been conditioned to believe in the importance of directness and sincerity, but Olivier valued a more disciplined self-presentation. If, to me, the definition of intimacy was letting it all hang out, to him that constituted a form of thoughtlessness. In the same way that Olivier liked it when I wore lipstick, or perfume—American men, in my experience, often claimed to prefer a more "natural" look—he trusted in a sort of emotional *maquillage*, in which people took a few minutes to compose their thoughts, rather than walking around, undone, in the affective equivalent of sweatpants. For him, the success of *le couple*—a relationship, in French, was something you were, not something you were in—depended on restraint rather than uninhibitedness. Where I saw artifice, he saw artfulness.

Every couple struggles, to one extent or another, to communicate, but our differences, concealing each other like nesting dolls, inhibited our trust in each other in ways that we scarcely understood. Olivier was careful of what he said to the point of parsimony; I spent my words like an oligarch with a terminal disease. My memory was all moods and tones, while he had a transcriptionist's recall for the details of our exchanges. Our household spats degenerated into linguistic warfare.

"I'll clean the kitchen after I finish my dinner," I'd say. "First, I'm going to read my book."

"My dinner," he'd reply, in a babyish voice. "My book."

To him, the tendency of English speakers to use the possessive pronoun where none was strictly necessary sounded immature, stroppy even: my dinner, my book, my toy.

"Whatever, it's *my* language," I'd reply.

And why, he'd want to know later, had I said I'd clean the kitchen, when I'd only tidied it up? I'd reply that no native speaker—by which I meant no *normal person*—would ever make that distinction, feeling as though I were living with Andy Kaufman's Foreign Man. His literalism missed the point, in a way that was as maddening as it was easily mocked.

For better or for worse, there was something off about us, in the way that we homed in on each other's sentences, focusing too intently, as though we were listening to the radio with the volume down a notch too low. "You don't seem like a married couple," someone said, minutes after meeting us at a party. We fascinated each other and frustrated each other. We could go exhilaratingly fast, or excruciatingly slow, but we often had trouble finding a reliable intermediate setting, a conversational cruise control. We didn't possess that easy shorthand, encoding all manner of attitudes and assumptions, by which some people seem able, nearly telepathically, to make themselves mutually known.

IN GENEVA, my lack of French introduced an asymmetry. I needed Olivier to execute a task as basic as buying a train ticket. He was my translator, my navigator, my amanuensis, my taxi dispatcher, my schoolmaster, my patron, my critic. Like someone very young or very old, I was forced to depend on him almost completely. A few weeks after the chimney sweep's visit, the cable guy came: I dialed Olivier's number and surrendered the phone, quiescent as a traveler handing over his papers. I had always been the kind of person who bounded up to the maître d' at a restaurant, ready to wrangle for a table. Now, I hung back. I overpaid and underasked—a tax on inarticulacy. I kept telling waiters that I was dead—*je suis finie*—when I meant to say that I had finished my salad.

I was lucky, I knew, privileged to be living in safety and comfort. Materially, my papers were in order. We had received a *livret de famille* from the French government, attesting that I was a member of the family of a European citizen. (The book, a sort of secular family bible, charged us to "assure together the moral and material direction of the family," and had space for the addition of twelve children.) My Swiss residency permit explained that I was entitled to reside in the country, with Olivier as my sponsor, under the auspices of "regroupement familial."

Emotionally, though, I was a displaced person. In leaving America and, then, leaving English, I had become a double immigrant or expatriate or whatever I was. (The distinctions could seem vain—what was an "expat" but an immigrant who drinks at lunch?) I could go back, but I couldn't: Olivier had lived in the United States for seven years and was unwilling to repeat the experience, fearing he would never thrive in a professional culture dominated by extra-large men discussing college sports. Some of my friends were taken aback that a return to the States wasn't up for discussion, but I felt I didn't have much choice. I wasn't going to dragoon Olivier into an existence that he had tried, and disliked, and explicitly wanted to avoid. Besides, I enjoyed living in Europe. For me, the first move, the physical one, had been easy. The transition into another language, however, was proving unexpectedly wrenching. Even though I had been living abroad—happily; ecstatically, even—for three years, I felt newly untethered in Geneva, a ghost ship set sail from the shores of my mother tongue.

My state of mindlessness manifested itself in bizarre ways. I couldn't name the president of the country I lived in; I didn't know how to dial whatever the Swiss version was of 911. When I noticed that the grass medians in our neighborhood had grown shaggy with neglect, I momentarily thought, "I should call the city council," and then abandoned the thought: it seemed like scolding someone else's kids. Because I never checked the weather, I was often shivering or soaked. Every so often I would walk out the door and notice that the shops were shuttered and no one was wearing a suit. Olivier called these "pop-up holidays"—Swiss observances of which we'd failed to get wind. Happy Saint Berthold's Day!

In Michel Butor's 1956 novel *Passing Time*, a French clerk is transferred to the fictitious English city of Bleston-on-Slee, a hellscape of fog and furnaces. "I had to struggle increasingly against the impression that all my efforts were foredoomed to failure, that I was going round and round a blank wall, that the doors were sham doors and the people dummies, the whole thing a hoax," the narrator says. Geneva felt similarly surreal. The city seemed a diorama, a failure of scale. Time unfurled vertically, as though, rather than moving through it, I was sinking down into it, like quicksand. I kept having a twinge in the upper right corner of my chest. It felt as though someone had pulled the cover too tight over a bed.

The gods punished their enemies by taking away their voices. Hera condemned Echo, the nymph whose stories so enchanted Zeus, to "prattle in a fainter tone, with mimic sounds, and accents not her own," forever repeating a few basic syllables. First God threw Adam and Eve out of the garden. Then he destroyed the Tower of Babel, casting humankind out of a linguistic paradise—where every object had a name and every name had an object and God was the word—in a kind of second fall. Language, as much as land, is a place. To be cut off from it is to be, in a sense, homeless.

Without language, my world diminished. One day I read about a study that demonstrated the importance of early exposure to language: in families on welfare, parents spoke about 600 words an hour to their children, while working-class parents spoke 1,200, and professional parents 2,100. By the time a child on welfare was three, he had heard 30 million fewer words than many of his peers, leaving him at an enduring disadvantage. I wondered how many fewer words I heard, read, and spoke each day in Geneva, deducting the conversations I couldn't make out; the newspaper headlines I neglected to absorb; the pleasantries that I failed to utter, from which serendipitous encounters didn't occur.

The back of our apartment overlooked a paved courtyard, where more senior residents of the building parked their cars. We didn't have air-conditioning. Neither did anyone else. In the evening, when the weather was hot, people retracted the yellow and orange canvas awnings that shrouded their balconies, rolled up the metal shades that kept their homes dark as breadboxes, and flung open their windows, disengaging the triple perimeter of privacy that regimented Swiss domestic life. Pots clattered. Onions sizzled. A dozen conversations washed into our kitchen, the flotsam and jetsam of a summer night. There were blue screens, old songs, mean cats. Somebody was serving a cake.

It was a disorientingly intimate score. This wasn't the suburbs. Nor was it New York, or even London, where alarm clocks were the only sounds you ever heard. Family life, someone else's plot, was drifting unbidden into our home. It slayed me—a reminder of all I wasn't taking part in, couldn't grasp, didn't know. Olivier took my melancholy as an affront. I was angry about being in Geneva, he calculated; he was the reason we were in Geneva; therefore, I was angry at him. He got defensive. I got loud. He would shush me, citing the neighbors, a constituency with which I had no truck. I felt as though I were living behind the aural equivalent of a one-way mirror. I didn't think that anyone could hear my voice.

BY LINGUISTS' BEST COUNT, there are somewhere between 6,000 and 7,000 languages—almost as many as there are species of bird. Mandarin Chinese is the largest, with 848 million native speakers. Next is Spanish, with 415 million, followed by English, with 335 million. Ninety percent of the world's languages are each spoken by fewer than a hundred thousand people. According to UNESCO's *Atlas of the World's Languages in Danger*, eighteen of them—Apiaká, Bikya, Bishuo, Chaná, Dampelas, Diahói, Kaixána, Lae, Laua, Patwin, Pémono, Taushiro, Tinigua, Tolowa, Volow, Wintu-Nomlaki, Yahgan, and Yarawi—have only a single speaker left.

The existence of language, and the diversity of its forms, is one of humankind's primal mysteries. Herodotus reported that the pharaoh Psammetichus seized two newborn peasant children and gave them to a shepherd, commanding that no one was to speak a word within their earshot. He did this "because he wanted to hear what speech would first come from the children, when they were past the age of indistinct babbling." Two years passed. The children ran toward the shepherd, shouting something that sounded to him like *bekos*, the Phrygian word for bread. From this, the Egyptians concluded that the Phrygians were a venerable race.

In the thirteen century, the Holy Roman emperor Frederick II performed a series of ghoulish experiments. According to the Franciscan monk Salimbene of Parma, he immured a live man in a cask, to see if his soul would escape. He plied two prisoners with food and drink, sending one to bed and the other out to hunt, and then had them disemboweled, to test which had better digested the feast. His research culminated with newborns, "bidding foster-mothers and nurses to suckle and bathe and wash the children, but in no wise to prattle or speak with them; for he would have learnt whether they would speak the Hebrew language (which had been the first), or Greek, or Latin, or Arabic, or perchance the tongue of their parents of whom they had been born. But he laboured in vain, for the children could not live without clappings of the hands, and gestures, and gladness of countenance, and blandishments." What happens when humans are prevented from acquiring language in the normal manner is impossible to know because it is unconscionable to facilitate—"the forbidden experiment."

Plato, Lucretius, Cicero, Voltaire, Rousseau, and Emerson all tried to explain, in one way or another, how languages evolved, and why there are so many of them. The question proved intractable enough that in 1865 the founders of the influential Société de Linguistique de Paris banned the discussion entirely, declaring, "The Society will accept no communication dealing with either the origin of language or the creation of a universal language." For much of the twentieth century the prohibition held, and the subject of the origin of language remained unfashionable and even taboo. Interest in language has resurged in recent years, alongside advances in brain imaging and cognitive science, but researchers—working in disciplines as diverse as primatology and neuropsychology—have yet to establish a definitive explanation of the origins and evolution of human speech. The linguists Morten Christensen and Simon Kirby have suggested that the mystery of language is likely "the hardest problem in science."

However people got to be scattered all over the earth, spouting mutually unintelligible tremulants and schwas and clicks, their ways of life are bound up in their languages. In addition to the various strangers with whom I couldn't interact in any but the most perfunctory of ways, there was Olivier's family, who now qualified as my closest kin by several thousand miles.

Olivier's brother Fabrice was thirty-two, an intensive care doctor in Paris. Their half brother, Hugo, was fifteen, a high-schooler near Bordeaux. They both spoke some English, but having to do so was an academic exercise, an exam around the dinner table that I hated to proctor. Their father, Jacques, a kind and raspy-voiced occupational doctor in Bordeaux, wrote beautifully—he'd studied English, along with German, in high school, and later taken an intensive course—but we had trouble understanding each other in conversation. I was unable to determine whether I considered Olivier's mother, Violeta, the ideal mother-in-law even though or because we were unable to sustain more than a five-second conversation in any language. A trained nurse, she worked as an administrator at a nursing home. She was the head of the local health care workers' union, and had recently led a strike in scrubs and three-inch heels. She and her second husband, Teddy, spoke no English whatsoever.

The first year that Olivier and I were together, Violeta sent a package from Nespresso as a gift for Olivier. It was a surprise, so she wrote to me, asking that I hide it away until his birthday.

The postman came. I signed for the parcel. As soon as he left, I proceeded to the computer, where I assured Violeta, quite elegantly, that I had taken delivery of the gift.

"J'ai fait l'accouchement de la cafetière," I typed, having checked and double-checked each word in my English-French dictionary.

Months went by before I learned that, by my account, I'd given birth to—as in, physically delivered, through the vagina—a coffee machine.

GROCERY STORES, as much as cathedrals or castles, reveal the essence of a place. In New York I'd shopped sparingly at the supermarket on my block—a cramped warren hawking concussed apples and a hundred kinds of milk. One day I bought a rotisserie chicken. I took it home and started shredding it to make a chicken salad. Halfway through, I realized that there was a ballpoint pen sticking straight out of the breast, like Steve Martin with an arrow through his head. The next day, receipt in hand, I went back to the store and asked for a refund.

"Where's the chicken?" the cashier barked.

"I threw it away," I said. "It had a ballpoint pen in it."

The closest grocery store to our apartment in London was almost parodically civilized. A cooperatively owned chain, it sold bulbs and sponsored a choir. Nothing amused me more than shaving a few pence off the purchase of a pack of toilet paper with a discount card that read "Mrs. L Z Collins." I'd hand it over to an employee-shareholder in a candy-striped shirt and a quilted vest, who would deposit the toilet paper into a plastic bag emblazoned with a crest: "By Appointment to Her Majesty the Queen Grocer and Wine & Spirit Merchants." If the store made a show of a certain kind of Englishness, its shelves were pure British multiculturalism: preserved lemons, *gungo* peas, *mee goreng*, soba noodles, lapsang souchong–smoked salmon. One November a "Thanksgiving" section appeared, featuring a mystifying array of maple syrup, dried mango chunks, and pickled beetroot.

As national rather than regional concerns, British supermarkets played an outsize role in public life. Every year, the launch of their competing Christmas puddings was attended by the sort of strangely consensual fanfare—everyone gets into it, even if it's silly—that Americans accord to each summer's blockbuster movies. The feedback loop of the food chain was tight: if a popular cookbook called for an obscure ingredient, the stores would quickly begin to carry it, a fact about which the newspapers would write, leading the cookbook to become even more popular, and the ingredient to materialize simultaneously in every British pantry. There was a coziness to the stores, amid their great convenience. Shopping in them always reminded me that London was a big city in a small country. From the £10 Dinner for Two deal at my supermarket—it included a starter or a pudding, a main course, a side dish, and an entire bottle of wine—I could extrapolate something about, and participate in, if I chose to, a typical middle-class British Friday night.

Food shopping in Geneva was a less idiosyncratic affair. For fruits and vegetables, I went often to the farmers' markets. They had nothing to do with yoga or gluten. They were just a cheaper place to buy better carrots. The selection, though, was limited. For everything else, there were the Swiss supermarkets—two chains distinguished, as far as I could tell, by the fact that one of them sold alcohol and the other didn't. I frequented the former, whose breakfasty theme colors made it seem like it was perpetually 7:00 a.m. Despite a few superficial points of contrast—you could find horse meat hanging alongside the chicken and the beef; the onions, taskingly, were the size of Ping-Pong balls—there wasn't much to distinguish the experience. Cruising the cold, clean aisles, I could have been in most any developed nation.

My nemesis there—my imaginary frenemy—was Betty Bossi, a fifty-eight-year-old busybody with pearl earrings and a shower cap of pin-curled hair. Betty Bossi was inescapable. There was nothing she didn't do, and nothing she did appealingly: stuffed mushrooms, bean sprouts, Caesar salad, Greek salad, mixed salad, potato salad, lentil salad, red root salad, "dreams of escape" salad, guacamole, tzatziki sauce, mango slices, grated carrots, chicken curry, egg and spinach sandwiches, orange juice, pizza dough, pastry dough, goulash, tofu, dim sum, shrimp cocktail, bratwurst, stroganoff, gnocchi, riz Casimir (a Swiss concoction of rice, veal cutlets, pepperoni, pineapple, hot red peppers, cream, banana, and currants).

Who was she? Where did she come from? What kind of name was Betty Bossi? Her corporate biography revealed that she was the invention of a Zurich copywriter, who had conjured her in 1956 in flagrant imitation of Betty Crocker. "The first name Betty, fashionable in each of the country's three linguistic regions, was accepted straightaway by the publicity agency," it read. "Equally, her last name was widespread all over the country. Together, they sounded good and were easy to pronounce in all the linguistic regions."

Switzerland, like Britain, was a small country, but due to any number of historical and geographical factors—chief among them the fact that the population didn't share a common language—it didn't have a particularly cohesive culture. The political system was heavily decentralized. (Name a Swiss politician.) There was no film industry to speak of, no fashion, no music. (Name a Swiss movie.) With the exception of Roger Federer, who spent his downtime in Dubai, there weren't really any public figures. (Name a Swiss celebrity.)

Swiss francophones looked to France for news and entertainment; German speakers gravitated toward Germany, and Italian speakers to Italy. (Speakers of Romansh, which is said to be the closest descendant of spoken Latin, made up less than 1 percent of the population and almost always spoke another language.) Gainful as it was, Switzerland's multilingualism rendered public life indistinct, a tuna surprise from the kitchen of Betty Bossi. The country was in Europe, but not of it. Its defining national attribute, neutrality, seemed at times to be a euphemism for a kind of self-interested disinterest. The morning after Russia announced that it was banning food products from the European Union due to its support of Ukraine, the front page of the local paper boasted "Russian Embargo Boosts Gruyère."

A few months later, it emerged that the supermarket chain that did not sell alcohol *was* selling mini coffee creamers whose lids featured portraits of Adolf Hitler. After a customer complained, a representative apologized for the error, saying, "I can't tell you how these labels got past our controls. Usually, the labels have pleasant images like trains, landscapes, and dogs—nothing polemic that can pose a problem." Betty Bossi as an icon; Hitler as a polemic. It was this bloodless quality that depressed me so much about Switzerland. My alienation stemmed less from a sense of being an outsider than from the feeling that there was nothing to be outside of.

The consolation prize of Geneva was the *grande boucherie*—a ninety-five-year-old emporium of shanks and shoulders and shins, aging woodcocks and unplucked capons, their feet the watery blue of a birthmark. The steaks were festooned with cherry tomatoes and sprigs of rosemary. The aproned butchers, surprisingly approachable for people of their level of expertise, would expound on the preparation of any dish. One day, craving steak tacos—Geneva's Mexican place only had pork ones, and a single order cost forty dollars—I convinced Olivier, who wasn't big on cooking, to chaperone me to the *boucherie.* I explained to him that I wanted to buy a *bavette de flanchet*, the closest thing I had been able to find to a flank steak, after Googling various permutations of "French" and "meat."

"Bonjour, monsieur," Olivier said. "On voudrait un flanchet, s'il vous plait."

The butcher rifled around in the cold case, his fingers grazing handwritten placards: *rumsteak, entrecôte, tournedos, joue de boeuf. Ronde de gîte, paleron, faux-filet.*

"Malheureusement, je n'ai pas de flanchet aujourd'hui," he said. "En fait, on n'a généralement pas de flanchet."

"What?" I said.

"He doesn't have a flank steak."

The butcher reached into the case and pulled out a small, dark purse of beef.

"Je vous propose l'araignée. C'est bien savoureux, comme le flanchet, mais plus tendre."

"What did he say?"

"He has an *araignée.*"

"What is that?"

"No idea. *Araignée* means spider."

"Okay, whatever, take it."

"Bon, ça serait super."

The *araignée* is the muscle that sheathes the socket of a cow's hock bone, so called because of the strands of fat that crisscross its surface like a cobweb. In francophone Switzerland, as in France, it is a humble but cherished cut. Different countries, I was surprised to learn, have different ways of dismantling a cow: an American butcher cuts straight across the carcass, sawing through the bones, but a French *boucher* follows the body's natural seams, extracting specific muscles. (American butchers are faster, but French butchers use more of the cow.) If you were to look at an American cow, in cross section, it would be a perfectly geometric Mondrian. A French cow is a Kandinsky, all whorls and arcs. You can't get a porterhouse in Geneva, any more than you can get an *araignée* in New York: not because it doesn't translate, but because it doesn't exist.

A flank steak, I would have assumed, is a flank steak, no matter how you say it. We think of words as having one-to-one correspondences to objects, as though they were mere labels transposed onto irreducible phenomena. But even simple, concrete objects can differ according to the time, the place, and the language in which they are expressed. In Hebrew, "arm" and "hand" comprise a single word, *yad*, so that you can shake arms with a new acquaintance. In Hawaiian, meanwhile, *lima* encompasses "arm," "hand," and "finger."

In a famous experiment, linguists assembled a group of sixty containers and asked English, Spanish, and Mandarin speakers to identify them. What in English comprised nineteen jars, sixteen bottles, fifteen containers, five cans, three jugs, one tube, and one box was, in Spanish, twenty-eight *frascos*, six *envases*, six *bidons*, three *aerosols*, three *botellas*, two *potes*, two *latas*, two *taros*, two *mamaderos*, and one *gotero*, *caja*, *talquera*, *taper*, *roceador*, and *pomo*. Mandarin speakers, meanwhile, identified forty *ping*, ten *guan*, five *tong*, four *he*, and a *guan*.

"The concepts we are trained to treat as distinct, the information our mother tongue continuously forces us to specify, the details it requires us to be attentive to, and the repeated associations it imposes on us—all these habits of speech can create habits of mind that affect more than merely the knowledge of language itself," the linguist Guy Deutscher has written. We don't call an arm an arm because it's an arm; it's an arm because we call it one. Language carves up the world into different morsels (a metaphor that a Russian speaker might refuse, as "carving," in Russian, can only be performed by an animate entity). It can fuse appendages and turn bottles into cans.

ALMOST AS SOON AS I'D arrived in Geneva, I'd begun to feel the pull of French. Already, I was intrigued by the blend of rudeness and refinement, the tension between the everyday and the exalted, that characterized the little I knew of the language. "Having your cake and eating it too" was *Vouloir le beurre, l'argent, et le cul de la crémière* ("To want the butter, the money, and the ass of the dairywoman"). *Raplapla* meant "tired." A *frileuse* was a woman who easily got cold. *La France profonde*, with its immemorial air, gave me chills in a way that "flyover country" didn't. I found it incredible that Olivier found it credible that the crash of Air France Flight 447 in 2009 could have been in some part attributable to a breakdown in the distinction between *vous* (the second person formal subject pronoun) and *tu* (the second person informal). Before the crash, the airline had promoted what was referred to in the French press as an Anglo-Saxon-style management culture in which employees universally addressed each other as *tu*. The theory was that the policy had contributed to the creation of a power vacuum, in which no one could figure out who was supposed to be in charge.

French was the language of Racine, Flaubert, Proust, and *Paris Match*. It wasn't as if I were being forced to expend thousands of hours of my life in an attempt to acquire Bislama or Nordfriisk. Even if I had been, it would have been an interesting experiment, a way to try to differentiate between nature and nurture, circumstance and self. Learning the language would give me a raison d'être in Geneva, transforming it from a backwater into a hub of a kingdom I wanted to be a part of. I wasn't living in France, but I could live in French.

As long as I didn't speak French, I knew that a membrane, however delicate, would separate me from my family. I didn't mind being the comedy relative, birthing household appliances, but I sensed that the role might not become me for a lifetime. There were depths and shallows of intimacy I would never be able to navigate with a dual-language dictionary in hand. I didn't want to be irrelevant or obnoxious. More than anything, I feared being alienated from the children Olivier and I hoped one day to have—tiny half-francophones who would cross their sevens and blow raspberries when they were annoyed, saddled with a Borat of a mother, babbling away in a tongue I didn't understand. This would have been true in any language, but I sensed that it might be especially so in French, which in its orthodoxy seemed to exert particularly strong effects. "Do you want to see an Eskimo?" Saul Bellow wrote. "Turn to the *Encyclopédie Larousse*."

Our first New Year's in Switzerland, Jacques and Hugo decided to visit.

"They said they want to come in the morning," Olivier told me.

"Okay. When?"

"In the morning."

"No, but when?"

"In the morning!"

Olivier, I could see, was starting to get exasperated. I was, too.

"What do you mean?" I said, a little too emphatically, as unable to reformulate my desire to know on which day of the week they would arrive as Olivier was to fathom another shade of meaning.

"What do you mean, 'What do I mean?' I meant exactly what I said."

"Well, what did you say, then?"

"I already said it."

"What?"

His voice grew low and a little bit sad.

"Talking to you in English," he said, "is like touching you with gloves."

Two

THE IMPERFECT

L'Imparfait

THE BELLS RANG every Wednesday morning. The teacher would lift the needle, drop the record on the spindle, and then:

> Frère Jacques, Frère Jacques,
> Dormez-vous? Dormez-vous?
> Sonny LaMatina, Sonny LaMatina,
> Ding dang dong, Ding dang dong.

I was five, a kindergartner. The song was pure sound, its hushed opening lines building to a pitter-patter and then to the crash-bang onomatopoeic finale that we liked to yell, hitting the terminal *g*'s like cymbals. The French teacher didn't force meaning on us. She let us revel in the strangeness of the syllables, which made us feel special, since we were only just old enough to be able to discern that they were strange. Sonny LaMatina sounded to me like an exotic but approachable friend. I imagined him as a car dealer, like the ones I had heard on WWQQ 101.3, Cape Fear's Country Leader: "Come on down to

Sonny LaMatina Honda Acura Mitsubishi. You can push it, pull it, or drag it in!"

The school occupied a low-slung brick building set back from the highway on a lot of sand and pine. I had lived in Wilmington, a beach town wedged between the Cape Fear River and the Atlantic Ocean, my entire life. My parents, who came from Philadelphia and Long Island, rendering them lifelong newcomers, had moved to North Carolina seventeen years earlier. My father was a criminal defense lawyer, handling everything from speeding tickets to murders. My mother worked from home—from our kitchen table, more precisely—tutoring high-school students in geometry and trig. We had a redbrick house, with green shutters and a picket fence. We knew exactly one person—a Korean-born woman with whom my mother played tennis—whose first language wasn't English.

I loved where I came from. Wilmington was anything but a soulless suburb. Its inhabitants proudly extolled its claims to fame—hometown of Michael Jordan, headquarters of the North Carolina Azalea Festival, the largest port in the state. *Dawson's Creek* was filmed there. The Venus flytrap, a carnivorous plant with leaves like the jaws of a rat, grew natively only within a sixty-mile radius. You could swim in March. June brought lightning bugs, and August, jellyfish: Portuguese men-of-war, sea wasps, cabbage heads.

My family's idea of a good vacation was to spend a week in a rented condominium 4.7 miles from our actual place of residence. My mother would drive home every day to water the grass. My brother, Matt, and I would ride bikes to a hot dog stand where the owner had shellacked a quarter onto the counter as an honesty test. We'd each get a North Carolina (mustard, chili, and slaw) and a Surfer (mustard, melted American cheese, and bacon bits), with pink lemonade that looked as if it had been brewed by dropping a highlighter inside a cup of water. Fall was oysters, roasted by the bushel and dumped on a table made from two metal drums and a piece of plywood, with a hole sawed out of the middle for the shells. When ACC basketball season arrived, church let out early. Teachers trundled televisions into the classrooms, blaring Dick Vitale.

People who live in big cities get people who live in small towns wrong: they don't want out. Wilmington was a place where people, considering their habitat unimprovable, tended to stay put. Only one member of my family had ever been abroad, once, but by local standards we were considered suspiciously urbane. We subscribed to the newspaper, which many Wilmingtonians detested, because it was owned by the *New York Times*. (A popular bumper sticker read "Don't Ask Me, I Read the *Wilmington Morning Star*.") We drove to Pennsylvania every year, in a Volvo, to visit my grandmother. (Another sticker, aimed at tourists: "I-40 West—Use it.") My parents encouraged us to pursue outside experiences. They were rarely illiberal, even in matters of which they had no direct knowledge. They were both keen readers, especially my mother, whose tastes in fiction were as sophisticated as they were simple in her everyday life. Their horizons were wider than those of many of the people around us, but they extended only a few hundred miles to the north.

Soon the school discontinued French in favor of Spanish, deeming it more practical. I became Laura, not Laurence. Roosters crowed *cocorico* instead of *quiquiriki*. On Wednesdays the record player crackled out "La Cucaracha" and, regardless of the season, "Feliz Navidad."

One day our English teacher asked us to write a poem. My parents found mine not long ago. They were coming to London for my wedding to Olivier, the night before which we were planning a big dinner in a pub. Yorkshire pudding was on the menu, and they weren't sure what it was.

My father flipped to the *Y* section of the family dictionary. A piece of loose-leaf paper fluttered to the ground. I had completed the poetry assignment with a fuzzy orange marker:

> I wish I could travel around the world, and s-e-e-e all
> the th-i-i-i-ngs.
> Oh, I would see all the countries and beautiful customs.
> Oh, I would see all the countries, Romainia Greece and
> all.
> I would see all the beautiful cultures. I wish I-I-I could.
> Oh, it would be so interesting. I wish I could travel
> around the w-o-o-o-o-rld. Oh!

THE FIRST PLACE I ever went was Disney World. We crammed into the car with one tape, Jack Nicholson and Bobby McFerrin doing Kipling's story about how the elephant, on the banks of the "great gray-green, greasy Limpopo River," got his trunk. The drive took nine hours: Myrtle Beach, where we stocked up on bang snaps and Roman candles; Savannah; St. Augustine; Daytona Beach. Finally, we arrived at Polynesian Village, a longhouse-style resort with koi ponds and a tropical rain forest in the lobby.

I pulled on tube socks and white sneakers and slung a purple plastic camera across my chest. Disappointment quickly set in. I was too scared to ride Space Mountain. Cinderella's castle held little allure—I was more interested in foreign countries than magic kingdoms. To a first-time traveler with dreams of high adventure, Main Street, U.S.A., seemed a scam, a staycation in the guise of a trip down memory lane. The windows of the shops were filigreed with the names of fake proprietors. I clocked a barbershop and some fudge kitchens. Where were the ziggurats, the cassowaries and the cuneiform tablets, the temples of marble and pillars of stone?

The next morning, we took the shuttle to Epcot. As we crossed into the Experimental Prototype Community of Tomorrow—even now, my impression of exoticism is such that the dome marking its entrance seems less a golf ball than a crystal ball, or at the very least a Scandinavian light fixture—I was transported, exported, by some freaky wormhole of globalization in which one could see the world by essentially staying at home.

We boarded Friendship Boats, approaching the World Showcase Lagoon on the International Gateway canal. We took a left into Mexico, where we rode a marionette carousel before proceeding southwest to the tea shops of China. We strolled around a *platz*. We listened to a campanile toll, saw the Eiffel Tower. We were after the epoch of Equatorial Africa (which Disney had planned, but never built) but before the dawn of Norway (whose pavilion would open in 1988, featuring a Viking ship and a stave church). Pubs and pyramids were coeval. Time seemed to scramble, as though it had been snipped up and pasted back together, like the map.

"All areas of Morocco are wheelchair accessible," the literature advised. In the medina, we followed the twang of an oud to a courtyard fragrant with olive trees and date palms. A belly dancer shimmied, her abdomen a bowl of rice pudding whose meniscus never broke. One of the musicians grabbed my hand and pulled me into a sort of conga line. Then and forever shy of crowd participation, I let completely, uncharacteristically loose.

French braid flying, I started doing something that would

have looked like the twist, were it not for the way I held my left leg in a *tendu*, the dutiful habit of a longtime ballet student. I was the center of a scrum of guys wearing scarlet fezzes. This, to me, was the magic kingdom. In Italy the Renaissance statues were hollow, impaled on metal rods to combat the Florida wind, and in Canada the loggers' shirts were made of mock flannel to combat the Florida sun. I didn't know. Simulations sometimes anticipate their simulacra. If I was ever going to go to Morocco, it was because I had already been.

IN THOSE DAYS my parents occasionally went away too. That fall they took the ferry with some friends to Bald Head, a barrier island known for Old Baldy, its defunct lighthouse. There were no cars there. It was a Saturday morning when my brother and I got the news that, the night before, my father had been thrown from the golf cart that he and my mother and their friends were riding in as it took a sharp curve, hitting his head on a concrete footpath. He was thirty-seven, in a coma. There was blood on his brain. Later, at Sunday school, one of my classmates—a miniature town crier in khaki pants and a blue blazer, lips ringed with doughnut powder—circulated a rumor that he had had too much to drink.

He had been the adventurer in our household, to the extent that there was one. In the summer of 1966 he had traveled to Madrid as part of a delegation from his Catholic boys' high school. One day he and a friend ditched their coats and ties and ran off to Gibraltar, where they hopped a boat to Tangier. The expedition yielded a sheepskin rug and twenty-one demerits, one more triggering automatic expulsion in the coming academic year.

The Marianist brothers of the Jericho Turnpike did not succeed, however, in stifling his curiosity about the world. He kept a list of every bird he had ever seen, dating from his days as a preadolescent twitcher, stalking the marshes of Alley Pond Park in Queens. Never mind that my father had been outside of America but once: he knew the capital of every country, the name of every river, which sea abutted what strait, how many countries were completely surrounded by other countries (three: Lesotho, San Marino, and Vatican City), why Chicago O'Hare's abbreviation was ORD (it used to be called Orchard Field).

By the time I'd started school, he was half of a two-man law firm that occupied a three-bedroom cottage a few blocks from the county courthouse. His office was my first foreign country: the wooden shingle hanging from the front porch, as though to mark a border crossing; the smell of cigarettes and correction fluid and shirt starch; the gold pens; the yellow pads; the zinging typewriter; the kitchenette drawers full of Toast Chees and Captain's Wafers and Nekot cookies; the sign behind the desk of Teresa, his all-powerful secretary, that read "I Go from Zero to Bitch in 3.5 Seconds." (Teresa was my first bureaucrat.) One of my father's clients, Marshgrass, paid him in grouper and bluefish. A judge named Napoleon Bonaparte Barefoot presided over district court. The language was crisp, formal, aspirated (affidavit, docket, retainer), and then demotic and slurry (a "dooey" was a Driving Under the Influence charge).

Each morning I helped my father pick out a tie, begging him, as we debated dots or stripes, to walk me through the day's cases. When friends came over for slumber parties, I'd insist that we try our Barbies for prostitution. As I understood it, prostitution entailed sleeping with someone to whom you weren't married. We often declared mistrials, in the knowledge that, having shared a bed, we were probably prostitutes ourselves.

At night I ran to the door, as eager as a sports fan to hear which cases my father had won, which he'd lost, how the bailiff had yelled at a defendant to get a belt. I often asked him to tell the story of one of his first trials, which concerned a man who had had the misfortune to be urinating in an alleyway where someone had recently broken into a car. A police officer approached and told him he was under arrest.

"What the fuck?" he said.

The police arrested him and took him to the station, where they put him in front of a witness, who said that the guy in front of him was definitely not the guy he'd just seen running away from the scene of the crime. The police charged my father's client anyhow, with disorderly conduct.

My father, just out of law school, spent a week in the library, trying to ensure that his client wouldn't end up with a criminal record on account of a single curse.

When the trial date arrived, the state presented its case. My father then rose and asked to approach the judge. Permission granted, he trudged toward the bench, carrying a leather-bound volume in which he had carefully marked the relevant law. Disorderly conduct, the book explained, had been committed only by a person who had said or done something that was "plainly likely to provoke violent retaliation," not by one who had merely spouted off a profanity without the expectation of a fight.

"I'd ask that you consider this statute—," my father began.

The judge took one look at the book and cut him off.

"That's *Raleigh* law, boy," he boomed, churning each syllable around in his mouth as though he were whipping cream.

My father retreated and, for lack of a better option, put his client on the stand.

"How many beers did you have?" the state's attorney asked.

"Nine," my father's client replied.

The judge banged the gavel, a woodpecker drilling bark. "Case dismissed! That's the only person who's told the truth in this courtroom all day long."

My father spun the tale beguilingly, transforming Wilmington into a low-stakes Maycomb, bandying between voices as though he were keeping rhythm for a crowd shucking corn. Now, after two decades in North Carolina, he sounded more or less like a southerner—an affectation, or an adaptation, that troubled my mother's conscience. "Your father's a chameleon," she would say, upon hearing him drop a *g* or leave an *o* hanging open like a garden gate. Changing the way you spoke, or simply permitting it to be changed by circumstance, constituted, in her view, a moral failing. It was weird, like wearing someone else's socks.

Her prejudice was an ancient one. To assume a foreign voice is to arrogate supernatural powers. In Greece, oracles prophesied fates and gastromancers channeled the dead, summoning monologues from deep within their bellies. In Hindu mythology, *akashvani*—"sky voices"—conducted messages from the gods. The book of Acts describes the visitation of the Holy Spirit as an effusion of chatter: "And suddenly there came from heaven a sound like a mighty rushing wind, and it filled the entire house where they were sitting. And divided tongues as of fire appeared to them and rested on each one of them. And they were all filled with the Holy Spirit and began to speak in other tongues as the Spirit gave them utterance."

In Paul's first letter, he tries to discourage the Corinthians from speaking in tongues, saying that it's better to speak five intelligible words than ten thousand in a language no one can understand. (In 2006, a study of the effects of glossolalia on the brain showed decreased activity in speakers' frontal lobes and language centers. "The amazing thing was how the images supported people's interpretation of what was happening," the doctor who led the study said. "The way they describe it, and what they believe, is that God is talking through them.") Muzzling charismatics, the early church established itself as the exclusive font of marvelous voices. By the Middle Ages, the ventriloquist was considered the mouthpiece of the devil. Like my father, he inspired fears of fraudulence. A sound-shifter, speaking from the stomach, not the heart, he might forget who he was.

Still, my parents schooled us in southern etiquette as well as they could, figuring that my brother and I had to grow where they had planted us. We said "Yes, sir" and "Yes, ma'am" to adults, even the ones who'd conceived us. My mother suppressed her cringes when the hairdresser called me Miss Priss. But she was proud of her northern upbringing and her Quaker education: she wasn't going to say that stuff herself. When my father traded "you guys" for "y'all," she saw an impersonator—a man with a puppet on his knee.

In 1954 Alan Ross, a professor of linguistics at Birmingham University, published a paper entitled "Upper Class English Usage" in the *Bulletin de la Societé Neophilologique de Helsinki*—a Finnish linguistics journal, borrowing prestige from French. In it, he cataloged U (upper-class) and non-U (middle-class) vocabularies, a taxonomy that Nancy Mitford went on to popularize in her essay "The English Aristocracy," asserting, "It is solely by their language nowadays that the upper classes are distinguished." U speakers pronounced *handkerchief* so that the final syllable rhymed with "stiff"; non-U speakers rhymed it with "beed" or "weave." The former might "bike" to someone's "house" for "luncheon," dining on "vegetables" and "pudding"; the latter would "cycle" to a "home" for a "dinner" of "greens" and a "sweet." Mitford elaborated on Ross's findings, playing expert witness to his court reporter. "Silence is the only possible U-response to many embarrassing modern situations: the ejaculation of 'cheers' before drinking, for example, or 'it was so nice seeing you,' after saying goodbye," she wrote. "In silence, too, one must endure the use of the Christian name by comparative strangers and the horror of being introduced by Christian name and surname without any prefix. This unspeakable usage sometimes occurs in letters—Dear XX—which, in silence, are quickly torn up, by me."

Wilmington had its own codes. Visitors were "company," a two-syllable word. *Coupon* was pronounced "cuepon"; the emphases in *umbrella* and *ambulance* were "UM-brella" and "ambu-LANCE." You "mowed the lawn," but you didn't "cut the grass." On a summer night, it was inadmissible to say you were going to "barbecue" or "grill"; you had to "cook out." A noun rather than a verb, *barbecue* was reserved for what most people would call—I can hardly write it now—"pulled pork."

Scientists say that in order to speak a language like a native, you must learn it before puberty. Henry Kissinger, who arrived in America from Bavaria, via London, at the age of fifteen, has an accent that a reporter once described as "as thick as potato chowder." His brother, two years younger, sounds like apple pie. My brother and I had spoken Southern from an early age. But as the offspring of Yankees, our peers reminded us, we existed on a sort of probation, forever obliged to prove ourselves in their ears. We endured as much teasing for the way our mother pronounced *tournament*—the first syllable rhyming with "whore," not "her"—as we did when my father, in a cowboy phase, broke both arms riding an Appaloosa, generating speculation during his convalescence as to who had wiped his ass.

. . .

BEFORE I WENT TO BED, my father and I would read. A scratch-and-sniff book was one of my favorite portals to sleep. I'd run a fingernail over a blackberry and find myself in a bramble, juice trickling down my chin. Turn a page, and my bedroom was a pizzeria, reeking of oregano and grease.

One night, as we inhaled, an unusual look wafted over my father's face. He asked me if he could take the book in to work with him the next morning. Sure, I said.

When his car rumbled into the driveway that evening, I flew down the stairs. I was waiting at the door when he came in the house with his jacket creased over his elbow, the sure sign of a win.

That afternoon, he said, he'd tried the case of a client who'd been charged with possession of marijuana. An officer had pulled him over, searched his car, and confiscated several ounces of an herbaceous green substance.

The only weakness in the prosecution's case was that the officer had failed to send the contraband off to the state crime lab for analysis. When he testified, my father had asked him to identify a sample of the substance.

"It's marijuana," the officer said.

"How do you know it's marijuana?"

"It looks like marijuana, it smells like marijuana. It's marijuana," the officer replied.

My father handed him my scratch-'n'-sniff book, open to a page that showed a rose in bloom.

"What does it look like?"

"A rose."

"What does it smell like?"

"A rose."

"Is it a rose?"

Juliet swore that a rose by another name would smell equally sweet. My father, by luring the officer into a converse fallacy—if marijuana, then herbaceous and green; herbaceous and green, therefore marijuana—was arguing that a "rose" wasn't always a rose. Both of them were getting at something about the fallibility of language. The great design flaw of human communication is the discrepancy between things and words.

Proper names, uniquely, work. Each one corresponds to a single object, meaning that if you say "Napoleon Bonaparte Barefoot," you're referring to a specific man, not to a set of people who share Napoleon Bonaparte Barefoot's characteristics. But words are basically memory aids, and if every particular thing had to have a unique name, there would be too many words for us to remember them all. Unless we were to heed Lemuel Gulliver's proposal—"Since words are only names for things, it would be more convenient for all men to carry about them such things as were necessary to express the particular business they are to discourse on"—a functional language must include words that refer to types of things rather than to each particular manifestation.

General terms are unbalanced equations. As abstractions, their correspondence is one to many, rather than one to one. In "An Essay Concerning Human Understanding," John Locke explored the dilemma, asking whether ice and water could be separate things, given that an Englishman bred in Jamaica, who had never seen ice, might come to England in the winter, discover a solid mass in his sink, and call it "hardened water." Would this substance be a new species to him, Locke asked, different from the water that he already knew? Locke said no, concluding that "our distinct species are nothing but distinct complex ideas, with distinct names annexed to them."

Three centuries later, the linguist William Labov took up the problem of referential indeterminacy, devising a series of experiments in which he showed a group of English speakers line drawings of a series of cuplike objects. Labov's experiment revealed that even among speakers of the same language, there was little agreement about what constituted a "cup" versus a "bowl," a "mug," or a "vase." No one could say at exactly what point one verged into the other. Furthermore, the subjects' sense of what to call the objects relied heavily on the situation: while a vessel of flowers might be called a "vase," the same container, filled with coffee, was almost unanimously considered a "cup."

Labov was building on a distinction that Locke had made between "real essences" (the properties that make it the thing that it is) and "nominal essences" (the name that we use, as a memory aid, to stand in for our conception of it). "The nominal essence of gold is that complex idea the word gold stands for, let it be, for instance, a body yellow, of a certain weight, malleable, fusible, and fixed," Locke wrote. "But the real essence is the constitution of the insensible parts of that body, on which those qualities and all the other properties of gold depend. How far these two are different, though they are both called essence, is obvious at first sight to discover." Replace *gold* with *marijuana*—a body green and herbaceous—and my father's point becomes clear: a rose is only a "rose," and "marijuana" is only marijuana, in a linguistically prelapsarian world, when the properties of a thing and its name are perfectly equivalent.

After his accident, my father remained in the hospital for weeks. Thanksgiving came and went—familiar food at a strange table. I was seven, child enough to be entertained by a makeshift toy: a plastic tray filled with uncooked rice. When he was well enough, I went to visit. A vague but specific imprint persists. A right turn from a corridor. Plate glass and a prone silhouette.

Terror came as an estrangement of the senses: a blindfold, a nose clip, a mitten, a gag. I remember only what I heard.

"Do you know who this is?" the nurse said, with the bored cheer of the rhetorical questioner.

He didn't, though. My father looked at me and committed a category error. Instead of my name, he said, "Bluebird."

TWO SUMMERS LATER I flung my sleeping bag—a red polyester number, embellished with parrots and palm fronds—onto the ticked mattress of the top bunk. I had pleaded to go to camp. At first my parents had resisted. But I kept on for the better part of a year, and eventually they agreed to send me, in the company of several hometown friends. For three weeks I would be drinking in the beautiful customs of Camp Illahee in the Blue Ridge Mountains of Transylvania County, North Carolina. Oh!

Illahee means "heavenly world" in Cherokee. The camp had been encouraging campers to "be a great girl" for nearly seventy years. It was an old-fashioned place, offering horseback riding, woodworking, archery, needlecraft, camping trips to crests that looked out on the deckled blue haze—it appeared to have been rendered from torn strips of construction paper—from which the range took its name. The ethos was brightly self-improving. According to the Log, the camp's collective diary, earlier generations of Illahee girls had been divided into three groups: "under five-three," "average/tall," "plump." A camper from 1947 wrote, "Vesta told us our figure defects and we found each other's. We studied the ideas of some of the world's great designers and found the clothes best suited for us."

By the time I arrived, the mode was Umbros and grosgrain hair bows. On Sundays we wore all white—shorts and a polo shirt buttoned to the neck, a periwinkle-blue cotton tie—to a fried-chicken lunch. Vespers was conducted in an outdoor chapel, nestled in a grove of pines. Each of us was allowed one candy bar and one soda per week. Swimming in the spring-fed lake was mandatory, as was communal showering afterward, unless you had swimmer's ear, a case of which I soon contracted.

The wake-up bell sounded at 7:45. I would sail through the morning activity periods, counting my cross-stitches and plucking my bows. But after lunch, when we repaired to our bunks for an hour of rest, my spirits would plummet. While my bunkmates jotted cheery letters to their families, I whimpered into my pillow, an incipient hodophobe racked by some impossible mix of homesickness and wanderlust.

Several nights into the session, I wet the bed. I told no one. Even with the parrots as camouflage, rest hour became a torture. Each afternoon I sat there, marinating in my ruined sleeping bag, convincing myself that catastrophes happened to people who ventured away from their hometowns. "COME GET ME! I can't make it three weeks," I wrote in a letter home. "I will pay you back, just take me away, please!"

THE PROGNOSIS, in the weeks that my father remained in intensive care, was that he would never work again. One day he got up out of bed and, ignoring the protests of his doctors, checked himself out of the hospital. He resumed his law practice the next week. His recovery was an act of obstinacy, an unmiraculous miracle attributable only to a prodigious will.

Still, it was hard when he came home. Like many victims of brain injuries, he was forgetful and paranoid. His temperament had changed; he was irrational where he'd been lucid, irascible where he'd once been calm. Even more confusingly, as the years went by, I had to take the fact of this transformation on faith from my mother—I'd been so young when it happened—mourning her version of a father I couldn't quite recall. The accident knocked our confidence, aggravating an already fearful strain in the family history. My mother coped with the situation, my brother accepted it, but I was furiously bereft. My desire to tackle Romania, or the Blue Ridge Mountains—my sense of confidence that I could, even—evaporated as I imagined my fate mirroring that of my mother, who was nine when her father had *his* accident.

John Zurn—she and her siblings always called him that, in the manner of a historical figure—had been the vice president of Zurn Industries. It was a plumbing products company, founded in 1900 by his grandfather, John A. Zurn, who had purchased the pattern for a backwater valve from the Erie City Iron Works. At thirty-four, John Zurn was a man of the world. As part of his prep school education, he had studied French and Latin. Now a tutor came to his office once a week to drill him in Spanish. Zurn Industries was counting on him, in the coming years, to take its floor drains and grease traps into Spain, Cuba, and Puerto Rico.

On December 3, 1959, John Zurn boarded Allegheny Airlines Flight 317, en route from Philadelphia to Erie. Attempting an emergency landing in a snowstorm, the plane slammed into Bald Eagle Mountain, near Wayne. The crash killed everyone aboard except for a sportswear executive, who declared, from his hospital bed, "The Lord opened up my side of the plane and I was able to jump out." As the *Titusville Herald* reported, John Zurn had been particularly unlucky: "Mr. Zurn boarded the ill-fated Flight 317 on a reservation listed by J. Mailey, who was coming to Erie to conduct business for the Zurn firm. Apparently last-minute plans were made for Mr. Zurn to travel to Erie in his place. Five children are among the survivors." The Maileys and their seven kids were my mother's family's next-door neighbors.

My grandmother, a thirty-one-year-old widow, remarried two years later. Her new husband was a cancer widower, with a girl and a boy of his own. Together they had two more children. In a photograph taken sometime in the mid-1960s, the brood, outfitted in floral dresses and bright sweater vests, is lined up by height—nine bars on a xylophone. Glimpsed through the window to the basement of the drafty fieldstone house on Fetters Mill Road, where children of various ages and provenances vied to become house champ in air hockey and foosball, or out on the snowy lawn, whooshing down hills on dinner trays, they might have been a poor man's Kennedys.

They were Protestants, though, descendants, on the Zurn side, of gentleman farmers who had immigrated from Zurndorf, one of the easternmost villages in Austria, to the Bodensee region of Switzerland. There, before moving to Philadelphia, they had been followers of Huldrych Zwingli, the reforming pastor who whitewashed the walls and removed the organ of the Grossmünster in Zurich. (I learned all of this only recently, reading an amateur genealogy produced by a great-uncle. Did I bridle at Geneva because I detected there something of my own congenital rigidity?) If trauma seemed to embolden the

Kennedys to the point of recklessnesss, it made my mother's family cautious. The ultimate wage of travel, John Zurn's death engendered in his survivors and their descendants a steadfast, preemptive provincialism—an aversion toward risk and adventure, which seemed to them indistinguishable.

MANY YEARS AFTER my father's accident, I learned that you can be less or more of a bird. Researchers asked college students to rate the "goodness" of different entities as examples of certain categories. Birds, in descending order of birdness:

robin
sparrow
bluejay
bluebird
canary
blackbird
dovc
lark
. . .
hawk
raven
goldfinch
parrot
sandpiper
ostrich
titmouse
emu
penguin
bat

I wondered how many words there were between a me and a bluebird.

In ninth grade I transferred to New Hanover, a public school of almost two thousand students. It had a football team and an on-campus cop, Officer Waymon B. Hyman. (Another great perk of a small-town upbringing is the names—one of our teachers was called Lawless Bean.) There was a new argot to master—a discriminating, and sometimes discriminatory, lineup of "thespians" and "yo-boys" and jocks and goths. The Catwalk was a caged overpass that connected the two main buildings. The Chafe was Lt. Colonel Chaffins, who patrolled the parking lots for truants. He directed the ROTC, which was supposed to stand for Result of Torn Condom.

I liked Hanover for its amplitude. The bell would ring and mayhem would break out, lockers slamming and kids screaming and screaming kids getting slammed into lockers. In my scaled-down universe—its topology distorted by homesickness, and the fear of experiencing it again, so that local became global, crowding great swaths of the world from view—Hanover was a teeming city after the village of private school. With a student body that was 50 percent white, 43 percent black, and 5 percent Hispanic, the school was significantly more diverse, but the atmosphere wasn't especially progressive. The school sponsored Miss New Hanover High School, a beauty pageant at which female students competed in evening gowns for a tiara. The homecoming queen was customarily white one year and black in the next one.

Some valiant teachers—Mrs. Bean, scandalously, had a tattoo—tried to expose us to life beyond our hometown and its strictures. An immovable rump of their colleagues, however, subscribed to the belief that book learning was poor preparation for the world as they knew it. To grow up in Wilmington was to have the invaluable privilege of belonging, of knowing that—whatever you did in your life—the same people who were there at its beginning would be there at its end. They were fixed points, forever findable. When the time came, they would welcome your children and mourn your parents. But the closeness of the community relied on its closedness, fostering a sort of micro-xenophobia, the threat less actual foreigners than people from other states. In Advanced Placement English, our teacher—with smudgy beauty mark and scrolled peroxide curls, rumored to be a former Playboy bunny—jettisoned the curriculum in favor of lessons in comportment.

"What is an appropriate hostess gift?" she would ask.

"A candle, a picture frame, or a box of chocolate," we chorused back.

"With what color ink should one compose a thank-you note?"

"Black is preferred for men, blue is preferred for women."

Tests were a breeze. All you had to do was walk to the front of the room and demonstrate that you could correctly enunciate words like *twenty* (not "twunny") and *pen* (avoiding "pin").

"Pop quiz!" she would cry, summoning one of us to the chalkboard like a game-show hostess waving down a contestant from the stands.

"What is the number after nineteen?"

"TWEN-ty."

"What is the number after nine?"

"TEN."

"What am I holding in my hand?"

"A PEN."

"All together now!"

"TEN PENS!"

A FEW YEARS LATER, southeastern North Carolina gave rise to its own neologism. It was 2003. France had just promised to veto the United Nations Security Council's resolution to invade Iraq. Neal Rowland, the owner of Cubbie's, a burger joint in Beaufort—two hours north of Wilmington on Highway 17—decided to strike back. A customer had reminded him that during World War I, sauerkraut makers had euphemized their product as "liberty cabbage," and frankfurters had been rechristened "hot dogs." Rowland bought stickers and slapped them on top of such menu items as fries and dressing, scrawling in "freedom" wherever it had once read "French." "At first, they thought I was crazy," he told CNN, of the employees of the restaurant's eleven branches across the state, as the stunt took off. "And then now, they think it's a great idea, and all the stores have started to change—Wilmington, Greenville, Kinston, all over."

In Washington, a North Carolina congressman urged his colleagues to join the "freedom fries" movement. Soon, the word *French* was purged from congressional dining rooms. The French issued an eye-rolling reply: "We are at a very serious moment dealing with very serious issues, and we are not focusing on the name you give to potatoes." They noted that *frites* were Belgian. Nonetheless, the trend caught on. The makers of French's mustard were forced to issue a press release: "The only thing French about French's mustard is the name." Aboard Air Force One, President George W. Bush's chefs served "stuffed Freedom toast," with strawberries and powdered sugar.

The next year, in the 2004 presidential election, Rush Limbaugh mocked John Kerry as Jean F. Chéri, a lover of Evian and brie. Tom DeLay, a wit of the era, began his fund-raising speeches with the line, "Good afternoon, or, as John Kerry might say, 'Bonjour.'" In 2012, when Mitt Romney—who had spent two years as a missionary in Bordeaux—ran for president, the trope that foreign languages, especially French, were unpatriotic remained in evidence. An ad entitled "The French Connection" was set to accordion music. It warned, of Romney, "And just like John Kerry—he speaks French." The gotcha shot was a clip of Romney saying "Je m'appelle Mitt Romney" in a promotional video for the Salt Lake City Olympics.

Foreign languages were not always taboo in America. The word *English* appears nowhere in the Constitution, whose framers declined to establish an official language. Many of them were multilingual. Perhaps they thought it obvious that English would prevail. Perhaps they were ambivalent about enshrining the tongue of their former oppressor in the foundational document of a nation that meant to overturn orthodoxies, welcoming men of varying origins.

English, in some sense, meant the monarchy, an association that gave rise to a number of revolutionary schemes. In 1783, when Noah Webster issued his blue-backed speller, freeing his countrymen to spell *gaol* "jail" and drop the *u* in *honour* (*spunge* and *soop*, sadly, never caught on), American English itself was a novel language, a runaway strain. One magazine justified it as the inevitable outgrowth of the dry American climate, writing, "The result is apt to be that the pronunciation is not only distinct, but has a nasal twang, which our English friends declare to be even more unpleasant than their wheeziness can be to us."

Americans were bursting with ideas about what language could be. They saw it as a church or a parliament, another institution to remake. Benjamin Franklin wanted to reform the alphabet so that each letter indicated a single sound. He invented six new letters including *ish* (to indicate the *sh* sound) and *edth* (for the *th* of *this*). A letter he wrote to demonstrate the system brings to mind a proto–I Can Has Cheezburger:

Ritsmɥnd, Dsulɥi 20.-68

Diir Pali,
Ɏhi intended to hev sent iu ꝺhiz Pepers sunɥr, bɥt biiŋ bizi fargat it.

The sound of America at its inception would have been lilting, susurrating, singsong, guttural. J. Hector St. John de Crèvecoeur, a French immigrant to New York, wrote in *Letters from an American Farmer*, his best-selling survey of revolutionary America, of "whole counties where not a word of English is spoken." In 1794, a bill that would have mandated the translation of official documents into German failed in the House of Representatives by a single vote. Dutch dominated the Hudson Valley, where the courts struggled to find English speakers to serve on juries. As François Furstenberg writes in *When the United States Spoke French*, Philadelphia was overrun with refugees from the French Revolution. During the 1790s, sixty-five Frenchmen lived on Second Street alone, including a Berniaud (china merchant), a Dumoutet (goldsmith), a Morel (hairdresser and perfumer), a Duprot (dancing master), and a Chemerinot (pastry cook). At the orchestra, audiences demanded that musicians play "La Marseillaise" and "Ça ira," leading Abigail

Adams to complain, "French tunes have for a long time usurped an uncontrould sway." In 1803, the Louisiana Purchase doubled the nation's French-speaking population. Louisiana entered the union as a bilingual state. Its second governor, Jacques Villeré, conducted the entirety of his official business in his only language: French.

Americans of the nineteenth century continued to accept linguistic pluralism as a fact of life. (Their tolerance notably did not extend to Native Americans, who were conscripted into English-only boarding schools, nor to slaves, whose masters forced them to speak English, while denying them the opportunity to learn to read and write.) During the Civil War, regiments such as New York's Second Infantry recruited soldiers with German posters—"Vorwärts Marsch!"—and maintained German as their language of command. Even as nativism surged in the 1850s, with the arrival of greater numbers of Catholic immigrants, the chorus persisted. In 1880 there were 641 German newspapers in the United States. (Even Benjamin Franklin founded a German newspaper, which failed after two issues.) One of them, *Pennsylvanischer Staatsbote*, had been in 1776 the first publication to announce that the Declaration of Independence had been adopted. English speakers had to wait until the next day, when the document's full text appeared in the *Philadelphia Evening Post*.

Twenty-four million foreigners came to America between 1800 and 1924. They hailed from different places than their predecessors: Italy, Russia, Greece, Hungary, Poland. In the West, the frontier was closing. In Europe, multilingual empires were giving way to monolingual nation-states, founded on the link between language and identity. As the country filled up, Americans of older standing began to cast doubt on the ability of the "new immigrants" to assimilate. In the *Atlantic*, a poem warned of "Men from the Volga and the Tartar steppes / Featureless figures of the Hoang-Ho, Malayan, Scythian, Teuton, Kelt, and Slav . . . In street and alley what strange tongues are loud / Accents of menace alien to our air / Voices that once the Tower of Babel knew!" In 1906 Congress passed a law precluding citizenship for any alien "who can not speak the English language." (According to the 1910 census, this amounted to 23 percent of the foreign-born population.)

World War I transformed bilingualism from an annoyance to a threat. As American soldiers fought Germans in the trenches, American citizens carried out a domestic purge of the "language of the enemy." In Columbus, Ohio, music teachers pasted blank sheets of paper over the scores of "The Watch on the Rhine." In New York, City College subtracted one point from the credit value of every course in German. Women's clubs distributed "Watch Your Speech" pledges to schoolchildren:

I love the UNITED STATES OF AMERICA.

I love my country's LANGUAGE.

I PROMISE:

1. That I will not dishonor my country's speech by leaving off the last syllables of words:
2. That I will say a good American "yes" and "no" in place of an Indian grunt "un-hum" and "nup-um" or a foreign "ya" or "yeh" or "nope":
3. That I will do my best to improve American speech by avoiding loud harsh tones, by enunciating distinctly and speaking pleasantly, clearly, and sincerely:

4. That I will try to make my country's language beautiful for the many boys and girls of foreign nations who come to live here:
5. That I will learn to articulate correctly one word a day for a year

By 1918, authorities in thirty-six states had passed laws forbidding the teaching of German. In a famous speech, Teddy Roosevelt laid down English as the criterion of belonging. "We have room for but one language here, and that is the English language, for we intend to see that the crucible turns our people out as Americans, of American nationality, and not dwellers in a polyglot boarding-house," he declared. In 1923 Illinois instituted American—*American*—as its official language. What began as subversion had become a shibboleth.

"I PLEDGE ALLEGIANCE to the flag of the United States of America, and to the republic for which it stands, one nation, under God, indivisible, with liberty and justice for all," we three hundred girls intoned.

"Let's try again," an older woman, clutching a microphone, commanded from the stage of the auditorium.

We were rising high-school juniors, "citizens" of Tar Heel Girls State, a weeklong seminar in representative government sponsored by the women's auxiliary of the American Legion. I had accepted the invitation under duress, having been led to believe that to decline the honor would lead to certain rejection by our great nation's institutes of higher learning. As delegates, we were meant to emulate a municipal government—writing a charter, empaneling a school board, electing a mayor. I hadn't ventured away from home since the humiliation of camp. As the terminus of my first foray out of self-imposed house arrest, the campus of UNC–Greensboro—and the mock city we were building within it—offered few of the enticements of Marrakesh, Florida. Name tags were mandatory. Parliamentary procedure was in effect. Housemothers ensured that residents didn't wear gaucho pants (I was never sure if I was wearing them or not) or speak to men (if we encountered one, say, working in the cafeteria, we were supposed to ignore him).

The proper way to say the Pledge of Allegiance, the woman explained—and the way it would be said at Tar Heel Girls State—was straight through, with no intake of breath before the divine prepositional phrase. We were to hold our elbows at a sharp ninety degrees, a sort of body-language analogue to not letting the flag touch the floor.

"Elbows up!" she bellowed. "Don't let them sag like chicken wings!"

"I pledge allegiance to the flag of the United States of America and to the republic for which it stands *one nation under God* indivisible with liberty and justice for all!" we yelled, triceps straining.

In *Meyer vs. Nebraska* (1923), the Supreme Court invalidated the conviction of a Nebraska schoolteacher who had read a Bible story to a student in German, but multilingualism never recovered its vitality. Before World War I, 65 percent of high-school students studied a foreign language. By the beginning of World War II, the number had dropped to 36 percent. (In Germany, Nazis condemned the bilingualism of ethnic minorities as a cause of "mercenary relativism." Hitler wrote that he failed to understand why the millions of Germans who were made to learn "two or three foreign languages only a fraction of which they can make use of later . . . must be tormented for nothing.") Desperate for linguists, the military enlisted Native Americans to develop and transmit messages. In the Pacific theater, Navajo code talkers flummoxed the Japanese—rendering "submarine" as *besh-lo* (iron fish) and "fighter plane" as *da-he-tih-hi* (hummingbird)—but their contributions went unrecognized for decades.

The launch of *Sputnik 1* in 1957 incited a linguistic arms race. Congress allocated funds for the expansion of foreign language programs, but the fervor was short-lived. In 1979 a presidential commission declared that "Americans' incompetence in foreign languages is nothing short of scandalous, and it is becoming worse." According to *The Tongue-Tied American*, a manifesto published by Senator Paul Simon to draw attention to the "foreign-language crisis," there were at the start of the Vietnam War fewer than five American-born experts—in universities and the State Department combined—who could speak any of the region's languages.

In 1981 S. I. Hayakawa, a Canadian born senator of Japanese descent, introduced the English Language Amendment: a proposal to consecrate English, once and for all, as the country's official language. The bill died without a vote, but its introduction marked the beginning of an era of renewed hostility to bilingualism. This time, the enemy was Spanish. In 1983 Hayakawa founded U.S. English, a lobby dedicated officially to "preserving the unifying role of the English language in the United States," and unofficially to making life miserable for immigrants of Hispanic origin. A decade after its establishment, U.S. English boasted 400,000 members and had spent $28 million persuading states to adopt its initiatives. These included forbidding 911 operators to speak in languages other than English. By 1990 seventeen states, North Carolina among them, had declared English their official language.

Supporters of U.S. English argued that foreign languages are like flotation devices, preventing immigrants from entering American waters unassisted. In reality, they buoy not only the prospects of their speakers—scientists have found that bilinguals enjoy a number of advantages, among them enhanced cognitive skills and lower rates of dementia—but also the ideals of the nation. In 1988 Arizona voters passed a referendum whose stipulations were so "overbroad," according to the judge who voided it, as to be incompatible with the First Amendment. Had the legislation held, municipalities such as Mesa, Casa Grande, and Ajo could have been forced to change their names. In the event, Navajo Nation threatened to exercise tribal sovereignty, restoring the names of tourist attractions like Monument Valley and Window Rock to Tsébii'nidzisgai and Tséghάhoodzáni.

Linguists call America "the graveyard of languages" because of its singular ability to take in millions of immigrants and extinguish their native languages in a few generations. A study of thirty-five nations found that "in no other country . . . did the rate of the mother tongue shift toward (English) monolingualism approach the rapidity of that found in the United States." Immigrants to America lose languages quickly; natives of America fail to acquire them. Only 18 percent of American schoolchildren are enrolled in foreign language courses, while 94 percent of European high-school students are studying English.

Since 9/11, monolingualism has seemed undesirable, and even dangerous. In the first three years after the attacks, the FBI more than tripled the funding of its language program.

Yet by 2006, of a thousand people who worked in the US Embassy in Baghdad, only six spoke fluent Arabic. Even as demand for education has increased, many school districts, battling budget cuts, have reduced their offerings. A double standard obtains: while learning a foreign language is considered prestigious, acquiring one naturally is stigmatized. We think of foreign languages as extremely hard to learn, but we're incensed when immigrants don't speak English perfectly.

Americans are by no means the first people to take an exceptional stance toward their language—in the sixteenth century the Dutch scholar Johannes Goropius Becanus became convinced that the original language happened to be the one he spoke, Antwerpian Flemish. Atatürk reformed Turkish under the auspices of the "sun language theory," which conveniently held that Turkish was the world's primal tongue, and that, since everything that had been imported into Turkish from other languages was really Turkish to begin with, Turks didn't have to get rid of all the foreign words they were already using. Early Irish grammarians asserted that Gaelic was superior to Latin because its parts of speech (noun, pronoun, verb, adverb, adjective, participle, conjunction, preposition, and interjection) mirrored the materials of the Tower of Babel (clay, water, wool, blood, wood, lime, pitch, linen, and bitumen).

The combination of the domestic protectionism of English and its international dominance, however, makes America one of the most linguistically isolated empires the world has ever known. "It's embarrassing when Europeans come over here, they all speak English, they speak French, they speak German. And then we go over to Europe and all we can say is 'Merci beaucoup,' right?" President Obama said on the campaign trail in 2008, confessing his monolingualism as a source of personal shame (even if, for electoral purposes, it was likely an asset).

The FBI, it emerged in 2015, had been subjecting many of its newly hired linguists to an "aggressive internal surveillance program," limiting their prospects for promotion. The criteria for inclusion in the program included foreign language fluency and ties abroad, the very skills for which they had been recruited. In the words of the film *Charlie Wilson's War*, the agency apparently didn't think it was "a good idea to have spies who speak the fucking language of the people they're spying on."

In 2009 Nick George, a student at Pomona College, was detained at the Philadelphia airport as he attempted to board a flight to Los Angeles. A physics and Arabic double major, he had spent the summer studying the language in Jordan. He was flying back to California to start his senior year. At the security checkpoint, an agent asked him to empty his pockets. When he handed over a stack of flash cards, the agent called in a supervisor.

"Do you know who did 9/11?" she asked.

"Osama bin Laden," George answered.

She asked him if he knew what language Osama bin Laden spoke.

"Arabic."

"So do you see why these cards are suspicious?"

OUR EDUCATION PERPETUATED the presumption of immobility, the map dot as lodestar. We took Spanish because it was theoretically useful in speaking to immigrants, which we never considered becoming.

One *profesora*'s pedagogical method consisted of sitting on a stool and announcing that she would be willing to field any questions. The room would often remain silent. This was an interrogation no one wanted to conduct. It was said that the *profesora* herself planted the tiny notes that proliferated, like fungi, in the crevices of the classroom's desks. Unfolded, they reportedly read, in English, "Ask Señora if she's pregnant."

Another *profesora* had been a fixture at the school since many of my friends' parents were students. During the summer she could be seen on the porch of her house, which overlooked the beach's main drag, surveilling the action from a rocker. Each Monday she began class in the same manner.

"¿Qué hicieron el fin de semana?" she would ask.

"Había una fiesta," somebody would reply.

"Qué interessssante," she would purr, clapping her hands, delighting in her success in extracting the weekend scoop under the guise of practicing the imperfect versus the preterite.

"¿Y qué pasó a la fiesta?"

"Josh *beso*'d Deanna."

"¿Es verdad?"

The *fin-de-semana* scuttlebutt would degenerate into a doubly substandard Spanglish and stretch until Friday. Atrocious pronunciation, accidental and deliberate, was indulged and even considered cute, especially for boys, especially for boy athletes, as foreign languages were thought to be a vaguely effeminate business. Failing to assimilate them was almost a form of good citizenship. We said "sacapuntas" a lot. We averaged a tense a year.

At Christmas the señora assigned us a holiday-themed art project, accompanied by an original composition. An array of half-baked handicrafts accumulated on her windowsill: ice-cream-cone Christmas trees, ragweed wreaths, droopy-faced elves fashioned out of bleach jugs.

The Friday before school let out for the holidays, a senior

named Jon—an avid sailor, with rimless glasses and a grizzled ponytail—showed up carrying a lumpy brown papier-mâché figure. With paws and a stripe on its back, it appeared to be some sort of rodent. (We later learned that it had originally been an art-class prairie dog, repurposed for the occasion.) On the top of its misshapen head, Jon had placed a miniature Santa hat.

Jon took his place in front of the class, clearing his throat. In a sonorous voice, he began to read:

El Castor de Navidad

Sentado, sonriendo, girando
Yo soy caliente y mojado.
Necesito el madero
Que Santa trae por la chimenea.

The Christmas Beaver

Sitting, smiling, gyrating
I am hot and wet.
I need the wood
That Santa brings down the chimney.

"¡Qué poema!" the señora cheered, breaking into rapturous applause. "¡Muy bueno!"

When the time came to think about college, I decided to apply to Princeton. It was an impulse: I liked the photograph on the front of the brochure, of a bicycle propped attitudinally against some arches. I knew that it would please my grand-

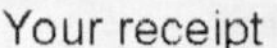

Your receipt

ALBANY LIBRARY

Customer Name: Shuen, Rachel

Items that you checked out

Title: When in French : love in a second language / Lauren Collins
ID: 31157053036464
Due: Tuesday, April 18, 2017

Total items: 1
Account balance: $0.00
3/28/2017 7:55 PM
Ready for pickup: 0

LIBRARY HOURS:
Mon 12-6, Tues-Wed 12-8
Thur 10-6, Sat 10-5, Sun 1-5

TO RENEW:

VISIT US ONLINE AT
www.aclibrary.org or

BY PHONE
Call 510-790-8096

mother, who lived nearby. (She was less excited by the link to John Zurn, who had matriculated there in 1942—his tenure was interrupted by the war—than she was by the lingering scent of Brooke Shields.) New Jersey, to me, might as well have been New Zealand. But reluctant as I was to leave home, I didn't want to follow many of my friends to college in North Carolina, where the hometown social lattice tessellated into a permanently inescapable statewide grid.

"I'm thinking of applying to Princeton," I told the guidance counselor. "Do you think I have a chance of getting in?"

"I'd say fifty-fifty."

"Okay?"

"Nobody's ever applied there. The best I can say is you might get in, you might not."

In mid-December I received an acceptance letter. That weekend we went to a Christmas party at the house of some family friends.

A man, the father of one of my classmates, approached, clutching a sweating Miller Lite wrapped in a shredded green paper napkin.

"Hear you're going to Princeton," he said.

I nodded, mentally preparing a humble reply to the congratulations that I imagined were forthcoming.

"Well, no matter what you do," he said, taking a swig, "don't get a Yankee accent."

Whatever horrors awaited, no one would have guessed that I would become an American living in Switzerland with a Frenchman I'd met in England. It was the longest of shots that I'd marry in a registry hall, under a portrait of the Queen, or that the grandparents of my children would be socialist nudists. I would be old enough to vote before I rode a train. My first passport, acquired when I was nineteen, reveals a tadpole-browed provincial in a lavender polo shirt and a red nylon anorak, newly acquired for the fall season from L.L. Bean. I'm jowly, grinning, with clothesline lips that will never properly nurture rounded vowels. I resemble a petite blond John McCain.

Three

THE PAST

Le Passé composé

THE PLANE LIFTED over wheat fields, terminal tanks, and shipping containers, gliding past the butterfly wing of the coastline, its edges fraying into foam. We had taken off from the airport near Honfleur, a fishing village in Normandy, where we had spent the afternoon eating lunch on the harbor, the wind rattling mainsheets like cowbells, before setting out to tentatively wander the streets of the old town, each of us trying to calibrate our pace to what we guessed was the other's level of interest in military souvenirs and producers of apple cider. It was just fall, the kind of day where summer lingers in the sun and winter lurks in the shade. It was our first time together as tourists.

We were flying at five thousand feet. The treacly dregs of daylight poured through the left side of the plane, where Olivier sat, manning the controls. I was next to him, forehead pressed against the window. The lower clouds were full, darkening to violet. Above them were *Cirrus uncinus*—mare's tails, glowing gold.

In half an hour we would land at White Waltham, a former RAF field outside of London, now a flying club where members could rent planes by the hour. That morning, as Olivier prepped for takeoff, calculating weights and checking gauges, I'd shoved damp palms into the pockets of my jacket. To abandon firm ground when you didn't have to struck me as a provocation. Olivier, from what I could gather, spent every second of his free time in the air. The home screen on his phone, I'd noticed, was a picture of a runway.

Snatches of air traffic control chatter occasionally flared from the radio. Otherwise, it was silent. We were quiet, too, holding hands. Below us, the sea was a sidewalk, the occasional ship a wad of gum. The sense of solitude was as luxuriant as if we had been lying under clean sheets in a king-size bed on the top floor of the tallest building in a city cleared of traffic. I was surprised at how calm I felt. We were alone, together, exactly halfway between France and England. I wondered where, at which exact ripple, La Manche gave way to the English Channel, *ciel* turned to sky, *la mer* became the ocean.

"Golf X-Ray Bravo Zulu Mike request frequency change to London," Olivier said into the microphone of his headset, breaking my reverie.

"Information one two three decimal seven five," the operator radioed back. "Zulu Mike frequency change approved. Squawk seven thousand."

Now we were flying over farmland, the grass like baize. Gliders swooped in the distance. Soon we would be descending.

"London Info, Golf X-Ray Bravo Zulu Mike," Olivier said. "Good afternoon. Requesting basic service."

"Golf X-Ray Bravo Zulu Mike, pass your message."

"Cessna 182, VFR flight with two people onboard from Deauville to White Waltham."

. . .

A YEAR EARLIER I'D been living in New York. Since leaving North Carolina, I'd traveled a little, but no one would have mistaken me for a jetsetter. When I was twenty-seven, the *New Yorker* assigned me to write a profile of the Italian fashion designer Donatella Versace. It was my first big work trip. I booked a ticket to Milan, and soon was sitting in the middle seat of the back row of an Alitalia plane, as anxious about pulling off the job as I was giddy at my luck.

Ten years earlier, Donatella's brother Gianni had been murdered by a serial killer on the steps of his mansion in Miami. In tribute to him, she had commissioned a ballet, to be performed at La Scala on the anniversary of his death. I sat in on rehearsals. Donatella, racked by nerves, hovered on the sidelines, fingering a skeleton key from the Miami house, the last thing Gianni touched before he died. That night I put on a gown, attended the ballet—a gunshot, a falling man in a red leather motorcycle jacket—and ate truffles in the cavernous staterooms of the Palazzo Reale. I wasn't able to choke down the espresso that followed, but neither did I expose myself as a complete yokel. The next morning, Donatella and a liveried driver picked me up from my hotel in a black Mercedes. We were to drive north, to visit the family's villa on the banks of Lake Como.

Donatella was in a philosophical mood. She had slept through the night, she said, for the first time in a decade. "I think change in life is important," she began, as the car wended its way into the hills above the city. "I don't like to look at the past. The past is inside you. Now, after ten years, this is a starting point for me to go towards something new."

It was July. She was chain-smoking. The air-conditioning

was off. With the tinted windows not so much as cracked, the air quality in the car was beginning to resemble that of a sweat lodge.

"Believe it or not, I have been listening to jazz at this moment, not rock," Donatella, still dilating on her newfound lightness of spirit, said as the chauffeur performed a stomach-churning swerve.

I felt my mouth water.

"I will die, Gabriele!" she yelled to the front seat. "No, he's a great driver. Ha-ha. *Bello!*"

We continued toward Como. Donatella was talking about her plans to spend August in the Caribbean. I knew I needed to ask her whether it was true that on vacation she typically brought along her own purple bedsheets, but I couldn't form the words.

"I'm feeling a little carsick," I finally whispered. "Maybe we should pull over?"

It was too late. Just as I croaked out my SOS, Gabriele shot into a tunnel.

At the villa, I was greeted by a manservant bearing a concoction in a crystal tumbler. "This is lemon water, without sugar," he commanded. "Drink it." I managed to conduct the interview, eating penne with caviar and touring a grotto. Donatella and I had been scheduled to ride back to Milan together, but something, I was told, had come up. The manservant hustled me into a van. Later I called my boyfriend. He didn't answer. I couldn't reach my mother, or anyone else. Panicking that I'd committed a firing offense, I dialed my father at his law office in North Carolina.

"Dad, I threw up on Donatella Versace."

"Honey, who's Donatella Versace?" he replied. "Is she one of your friends?"

. . .

Soon I was twenty-nine, newly dumped. For several years I'd been dating an Englishman who had two middle names and wore lavender socks. His residence in my life, before Olivier, might lead one to believe that I was partial to foreign men. But in fact he was the latest entry in a catalog of relationships that, taken in the aggregate, made absolutely no sense. My first boyfriend, in high school, had been a "yo-boy": that was how "preps" like me referred to the skaters and surfers, who wore hooded sweatshirts, drove cars that were low instead of high, and shunned jam bands for rap. After that I went out with a "baseball player," another local genre. They were country boys, chewers of dip and drinkers of Mountain Dew, who had part-time jobs delivering bottled water, cut the sleeves off their T-shirts, and lived in ranch houses with American flags flying out front.

In college I fell in love with a tall Tennessean who directed his considerable intellectual gifts largely toward gambling on sports. The son of a southern lawyer and a serious-minded northern mother, he was so much like me: a partier and a reader, as introverted as he was sociable, stuck between two parts of himself whose ambitions and desires often seemed to be in direct opposition. He was a fraternity stalwart. He was also a bagpiper, a history nut, a brilliant writer, a real friend to many women. I couldn't assimilate these contradictions any more than I could my own. I was always giving him horrible gifts—a clan Houston cummerbund and bow tie, when he'd have preferred a Coetzee novel—trying to push him toward one pole of his identity, to make him into a type, as typical as possible. I felt I lacked a culture: I was a WASP, but I wasn't a WASP; I was Irish Catholic, but I wasn't Irish Catholic; I was southern, but I wasn't southern. Dating a person who had one, or strong-arming him into one facet of it, I could be someone by proxy. I was always looking for more of a bird.

Not long after the Englishman and I broke up, a friend from college invited me to a party, an "urban tailgate" in Madison Square Park. There would be Frisbee, the e-mail promised, and Jell-O shots. Fun would be had by all. That sounds like a terrible party, I thought. I went anyway, heeding the immortal rule that to refuse an invitation, as a single person, is to invite the misery for which you're sure you're destined. It was a terrible party. I quietly fled to a nearby restaurant, where I found a seat at the bar.

Eating a steak and drinking a glass of red wine by myself, I was significantly less miserable than I had been half an hour earlier. If I can tolerate some level of solitude, I thought, why am I here in Flatiron, eating dinner alone, instead of off somewhere having an adventure? A long-suppressed, late-breaking desire began to rise within me. It was as though someone had stuck a pipette into my id and squeezed the bulb. I loved New York, and I loved my job, but I had spent every day of my working life reporting for duty at the same desk. I was an organization kid, aging out of the period in life that indulges experimentation. I had never really taken a risk.

NINE MONTHS LATER, thanks to a kind boss and portable profession, I arrived in London, a city I'd chosen largely on the basis of the fact that I, like its inhabitants, spoke English. My possessions whittled to the contents of two duffel bags, I showed up and proceeded to the studio apartment that I'd signed for, unseen, on the recommendation of an acquaintance.

It was perfect: clean, white, cold, with high ceilings and that London-flat smell of radiators, carpet, and mail. Wooden shutters as tall as barn doors flanked a pair of French windows that opened onto an overgrown balcony with a wrought-iron railing. The move seemed fated. Later, people would ask what kind of visa I had, and how I'd managed to secure it, and who had been my lawyer. I'd just gone on the website and filled out some forms. The documents had arrived not long after, as though I'd ordered a pizza.

I assumed I would stay a year or two, eat some scones, move back to New York. Meanwhile, I basked in the parks and parapets, the blue plaques and stained palaces, the roads that bore the names of the places to which they led, having been furrowed, long before the rubber tire, by feet and wheels and hooves. I'd never had a garden, or even a cactus, but on the balcony I dug dead plants out of concrete urns and potted boxwoods, lavender, a gardenia. I cleared out a window box and soon had a free supply of basil.

Mornings, I rode a bike to the London Library, where I worked at a long table in a pleasantly fungal room presided over by a bust of Hermes of Praxiteles. The actress who played Karen, the wife on *Californication*, often sat beside me, typing with surprising fervor. (I later found out that she'd been married to a surgeon who, coming home late from an operation, had dropped dead on their doorstep. Pregnant with their third child, she continued to write letters to him, which she eventually published.) I liked how you could be more than one thing in London, how industries intermingled and demographics mixed. I took trains to the countryside and exercised my right to ramble, keeping the hawthorn trees on my right-hand side, passing through kissing gates. I learned to cook. I went to a picnic where an elderly woman took a look at my feet and said, "Red shoes, no knickers." Then I realized that she was wearing orthopedic sandals the color of a tomato.

London seemed, from the start, a deeply tolerant place, whose forbearance yielded freedom without giving off the usual urban by-product of aggression. History had discredited the flag-waving impulse, so—at least for foreigners, who were exempt from the strictures of the class system—the greater part of fitting in was showing up. Going to the gym was considered a harmless but slightly embarrassing activity, like philately or folk dancing. People didn't put their phones on the table during dinner, and if you droned on about your job or your kids or your diet, they didn't feign interest. It seemed both easier and more intense. If New York was the movies, London was the boxed set.

The city was familiar but intriguing, the friend of a friend. Newspapers were trashy, but television was dignified. Lunch was dinner, where whoever you were eating it with would most often encourage you to join him in a "cheeky glass." Chief among the city's charms, for me, was the vibrancy of British English—the blunt pejoratives, the thrusting staccato verbs. Knobs, yobs, wankers, berks. Sack, shag, chuff, nick. The word *bellend* was the most efficient synecdoche I'd ever heard.

In public speech, trying to be memorable and coming off as slightly unhinged remained more advantageous than trying to be bland and succeeding. The Houses of Parliament had eleven bars, one of which had an arrow near the exit, three inches from the ground: "It is to accommodate those who choose to leave the premises on their hands and knees," a police officer once told a reporter. The month I arrived, an MP named Mark Reckless went on a six-hour binge and missed the vote on the budget. "I'm terribly, terribly embarrassed," he said. "I apologise unreservedly and I don't plan to drink again *at Westminster*." (Italics mine.)

This was a city whose "love-rat" mayor once dismissed rumors of an affair as "an inverted pyramid of piffle," the intellectual arsenal of a country where words were deployed like darts. There was an entire church—St. Bride's, designed by Sir Christopher Wren in 1672—dedicated to journalists. My supermarket published its own surprisingly good magazine, which I would flip through while enjoying the slatternly pleasure of "having a lie-in." On the radio one atypically rainless Saturday morning, I heard the weatherman prophesying "a usable day."

A sort of two-for-the-price-of-one city, London was one of the world's great conglomerations of buildings and roads and restaurants and theaters and people, overlaid by an equally superb megalopolis of words. British English was my gateway language. I strolled in the mews of understatement. I drove the wrong way down the streets of *graft* (meaning "hard labor," rather than "corruption") and *quite* (meaning "not very" rather than its opposite). I stalled in the roundabout of the English non sequitur, in which someone declares that something is dreadful and ghastly—this usually involves boarding school, or Wales—and then says immediately, "It was great fun."

Lamenting the way that the uprootedness of the New World manifested itself in the American vocabulary, Edith Wharton asked, "What has become, in America, of the copse, the spinney, the hedgerow, the dale, the vale, the weald?" If my infatuation was not requited—one day I opened a newspaper to find a letter from a man furious that his local convenience store had "seemingly used a foreign dialect of the English language to describe biscuits as 'cookies'"—it was invigorating. I reveled in plural collective nouns ("England are winning") and pro-predicates ("They might do"), the joy of experiencing my own language at a ten-degree remove.

I SAW A FACE ACROSS the room—deep-set hazel eyes, nose like an arrowhead. It was, unmistakably, a European face. Why, I wondered—as I'd wondered many times on the subway in New York, playing an idle game in which I tried to figure out where my fellow passengers had come from, whether recently or long ago—were Europeans in Europe immediately distinguishable from the many Americans who shared their genetic material? Even controlling for environmental factors—nutrition, dentistry, haircuts, red glasses—there seemed to be something different in the strength of the features, the splay of the crow's-feet, the hold of the jaw. All four of my father's grandparents were born in Ireland, but you could dress him in a flat cap and tweeds and still pick him out of a lineup. The dimple that slashed from the cheek to the chin of the person I was staring at seemed almost like a geographical feature, a gully that had taken centuries to carve.

I'm in Europe, I thought, with all the discernment of a study-abroad student determined to have chow mein on her first night in Beijing. I'm going to go talk to that European man!

I accosted him, sticking my hand out and stating my name in a manner that I would later learn is considered, by people who are not Americans, to be fairly bizarre.

He introduced himself as Olivier.

I asked where he was from. He was French, he said, from a beach town near Bordeaux.

"It sounds a lot like Wilmington," I replied.

Amazingly, he knew what I was talking about. He'd once

been to my hometown, for the wedding of a North Carolinian he had befriended while studying in the US. It was probably the first time I had ever spoken more than a few words to a French person (or, for that matter, to a mathematician), but he seemed immediately familiar. We categorize people by the hemispheres they inhabit, the continents they occupy, the countries they live in, the deserts they traverse. Why not classify them by their affinities to oceans? If land were water, Olivier and I were compatriots. Swap blue for green as the organizing principle of the map, and we came from the same *terroir.*

We sat down. Neither of us knew the host of the party, which was taking place in an apartment above a Polish restaurant. Olivier had tagged along with some French acquaintances. I had come with some friends of a friend, Americans and Australians whom I had never met before and would never see again. I had been in London for twenty-one days.

A bottle of wine was sitting on the coffee table. Olivier glanced at the label before pouring it, dripless, into two dentist-size plastic cups, a move that struck me as the height of Continental refinement. We kept talking. I was surprised when he got up and said he had to leave. He was exhausted, he explained, from having spent the day at the airfield practicing aerobatics. As he spoke, he unconsciously mimed the maneuvers: stalls, barrel rolls, Cuban 8s.

A few days later, I got an e-mail asking if I wanted to get a drink.

"I'd like that," I wrote back. "You can fly me to the pub."

He suggested a place.

"C'est bon!" I replied.

I now know that this means "It's good!"

We met on a Tuesday night. Petunias blared like phonographs from the pub's facade. Inside, there were oriental rugs and flocked wallpaper. We squeezed onto benches at a long, sticky wooden table. Next to us, a couple was having an animated conversation, which seemed to involve something called a "budgie smuggler."

"What's a budgie smuggler?" I whispered to Olivier.

"No idea," he said. (With his accent, it came out sounding like he was lacking identification.)

He turned to the man on his right, polite as could be.

"Excuse me, but we were wondering about budgie smugglers?"

The man was happy to give us a lesson. A budgie smuggler, he explained, was a bikini swimsuit for a man, so called because it gave the impression of its wearer having shoved a budgerigar—it sounded like a lawnmower, but it meant a parakeet—down his pants. *Budgie smuggler*: the first entry in our private thesaurus. We bought the next round.

Olivier asked if I wanted to get dinner. He had made three reservations. I chose Chinese. Soon I was living with a man who used Chanel deodorant and believed it to be a consensus view that Napoleon lost at Waterloo on account of the rain.

WE SPOKE TO EACH OTHER in endearments. My darling, my love, *mon amour*, *ma chérie*, *poussin*, *mouton*, *bébé*. This was new to me, not characteristic. The word *baby*, applied to anyone over two, had always seemed like the adult diaper of endearments.

"*Mon amour*," he'd say. "Pass me the salt?"

I'd yell across a store, trying to get his attention: "*Bébé!* Over here, in dairy products."

People we knew, I think, made fun of us. What they didn't know was that we couldn't say each other's names.

In 1661, deeply in debt, Racine set out on horseback for Uzès, in southeastern France. He was hoping that his maternal uncle, who served as vicar general to the city's bishop, could help him get a job. A Parisian, Racine spoke Francien, the predecessor of modern French. Once he reached Lyon, where the Franco-Provençal language prevailed, he could no longer make himself understood. "This misfortune got worse at Valence," he wrote to a friend, "for God willed it that I asked a maid for a chamber-pot and she pushed a heater under my bed. You can imagine the consequences of this damned adventure, and what happens to a sleepy man who uses a heater for his night-time necessities." By the time Racine reached Uzès, he wrote, "I can assure you that I have as much need of an interpreter as a Muscovite would in Paris."

Nine months after we'd met, Olivier invited me to Bordeaux for Easter. We arrived on Good Friday, picked up a rental car at the airport, and drove into the city for lunch. Olivier showed me the hospital where he was born; the apartment where he had lived during cram school; the bars where he and his friends had hung out as students; the crack-of-dawn fish market where, after the bars, they had once bought a whole octopus to shove into the mailbox of a classmate who'd gone home early. That afternoon we followed the right bank of the Gironde estuary east to the vineyards—in the fall, Olivier said, surfers got into the river, paddled to the middle, and rode a waist-high tidal wave called the *mascaret*.

In Saint-Émilion, we stopped at the first vineyard we saw.

A sprightly man with a crooked smile greeted us at the end of the drive. Introducing himself as the estate's proprietor, he led us into a musty *cave*.

"I inherited the vineyard from my father, who inherited it from his father," he told us, pouring some wine. "But my true passion is magic."

We tasted the wine. It was good, for the product of a man who would rather be locking people in a box and sawing them in half.

"Fortunately I married the perfect woman," he said. He gestured out the window toward a hunched-over figure in the fields.

"That's my wife," he said, beaming. "She's a certified oenologist."

Before leaving, we bought a few bottles to take to Olivier's parents. I thought about the reluctant vigneron's fantastically sensible marriage, how he had retrofitted his life with someone whose skills exactly matched his specifications. As he was making change, he pulled one of the minor Euro coins out of my ear.

At last: time to meet Les Fockers. I fidgeted all the way to Andernos-les-Bains, the village where Violeta and Teddy lived. Olivier had assured me that they were adorable (even though the words are identical, the French version seemed more genuinely affectionate, free of the patronizing edge of its English counterpart, and somehow less gendered: I couldn't imagine an American male saying "adorable," a habit I thus found adorable itself). Still I was nervous, the usual anxieties a person has about whether or not her boyfriend's family will like her overlaid with uncertainty as to whether, in the fog of language, they'd even be able to make out the right person to like or not.

I'd never been a francophile, much less a francophone. If I'd had to free-associate about the French, I might have said, unimaginatively: cheese, scarves, rude. Before I met Olivier, my most intensive exposure to the language had occurred during ten days I'd spent camping in the Sahara, on assignment with an American photographer and his crew. The Algerians—half a dozen young men who spoke Tamasheq, Arabic, and French—had been superb company, despite the language barrier. But they simply had not been able to figure out what I, an unaccompanied woman, was doing there in the middle of the desert. Neither of the two words I knew in French, *oui* and *non*, had seemed exactly the right answer to their repeated enquiries as to whether I was a virgin.

We parked on the street outside Violeta and Teddy's house, a bungalow on a quiet boulevard. Before Olivier even pulled the keys out of the ignition, they'd come running out to greet us. Violeta, in a platinum-blond side ponytail and purple heels, covered us both in kisses. Her tangerine-colored lipstick left imprints all over my cheeks, like the franking on an international package.

Teddy, seventy-eight and immaculate, insisted on carrying our luggage. We passed through the front yard. There was a hammock, a patio covered with artificial turf, hummingbird feeders, hibiscuses. Inside the house, ruby-colored beads dangled from a chandelier. A Venetian mask hung near a tasseled lampshade. The entryway was dominated by an antique bureau, covered in lace and porcelain figurines and incense sticks, which, after our marriage, would be replaced with a huge collage of wedding pictures in a heart-shaped frame that Teddy had painted.

I handed Violeta a box of chocolates.

She led us to our bedroom, where a package was sitting on the desk.

"Merci!" I said, fumbling with the wrapping. "Merci beaucoup!"

It was Miss Dior Chérie, my first bottle of perfume.

That night, we drove around the Arcachon Bay to Cap Ferret, at the tip of the peninsula. I knew the landscape like a friend's face: the flat-cheeked marshes, stubbled with sawgrass and pocked with hermit crab holes; the sugary topsoil of the pine forests, which a bike could hardly grip. Flats of pluff mud let off a sweet hypoxic reek. The air was low and clammy, as though someone had smothered the horizon with a wet paper towel.

The sun was going down as we arrived at an open-air bar—striped umbrellas and some tables in the yard—run by a friend of Fabrice's, a third-generation oyster farmer. Fabrice was in Paris working, but the rest of the family had gathered: Jacques; Hugo; Marie, Hugo's mother. Jacques looked so much like Olivier. He was shy, but expressive, with a poetic way of phrasing things. "I pray you!" he'd tell me, clasping his hands, his English version of *je vous en prie*, when he wanted to emphasize a point. Wrapped in fleece blankets, we toasted to health. The wine came from Bordeaux. The oysters came from the far side of Mimbeau, a sandbar that jutted out from the cape, two hundred feet from where we sat. It was low tide. The thin wooden poles that supported the oyster beds wavered against the sky like rubber pencils.

After the apéritif—the pregame show to the French family meal—we proceeded in caravan formation to Jacques and Marie's. As soon as we sat down for dinner, the table exploded into chatter, followed by rebuttal, counterargument, rejoinder. That was my impression, at least, judging from the unsmiling looks, the disputatious *mais nons*, the blowing of air out of cheeks. I wasn't sure whether, or when, resolutions came. I felt like an explorer picking her way through a jungle, turning toward stimuli as they chirped and hooted. The language came in an oxytonic rush. It sounded to me like heavy rain, sluicing down a roof.

Listening to Olivier speak French was a bizarre sensation. I felt as though he had thrown on a jersey, sprinted onto the field, and proven himself a skilled player of a sport to which I did not know the rules. I was impressed by his mastery of the game, but alienated by my ignorance of it. The primal fantasy of intimacy is a secret language—one in which only the two of you can talk. French reinforced the primacy of preexisting bonds over the ones that we had built. It was a sort of conversational clubhouse, a pig Latin of which I was the odd woman out.

I retreated to the linguistic version of a kids' table—giggling in international pop-cultural English with Hugo. My thoughts wandered, mainly to what sort of impression I was silently making. Unable to present myself the way I would have liked to, I felt exposed, as though I'd been rousted from bed and dragged to a party, forced to come as I was. But the passivity was also liberating: a free pass from the obligation of attempting to be intelligent, witty, or well informed. It made me consider whether there was some ineffable part of a person that transcended socialization, an essence that remained once the top notes of politesse faded off. Could Olivier's family smell something fundamental about me, and if so, what was it? What did I exude when I couldn't talk?

As much as I worried about how they would judge me, my impulse to judge them seemed to have evaporated with my powers of articulation. My critical faculties in abeyance, for once, I simply thought, What kind people, what a good meal, and how warm a reception. Violeta reminded me in many ways of my own mother: full of energy, unstudied, and unserious about herself, but formidable in her willingness to go to any length to ensure her children's success. They were both the kind of parents who had jumped out of bed in the middle of the night to encourage safe passage from teenage parties; who would meet a plane at any far-flung airport at any inconvenient hour; who were always trying, even if we could now afford it better than they, to pay for our flights. If Violeta had a daughter, I was sure she would greet her as my mother did me every time I came home, stripping herself of necklaces and sweaters and pairs of shoes at the slightest expression of admiration; running up the stairs to plunder her own closet before knocking on my bedroom door; forwarding everything I wrote to her family and many friends, never with less than a dozen exclamation points; accepting, and even applauding, the fact that I had moved halfway around the world, because she only ever thought of my happiness, not hers.

I was rarely able to appreciate my own mother's ebullience, though, without criticizing her unworldliness. I sometimes found her naïveté its own form of affectation. It struck me as stunted that she had never smoked a cigarette, eaten a bite of fish, gone to a restaurant by herself, mixed her own drink. The joke in our family went that she had invented sushi, having—one Valentine's Day in the 1970s—served up a cocktail dish of gelid gray shrimp, not realizing that they were supposed to be cooked. For his part, my father had neither a computer nor an e-mail address, cell phone nor ATM card, such was the fixity he required of the world. As much as I depended on my parents' constancy—their permanent address, their forty years of marriage, their perpetual availability, their diligence in hanging on to immunization records and school diplomas—I faulted them for a lack of imagination. But at Olivier's family table, deprived of the tools of discernment, I didn't have the option to be cutting. I felt like a fool, but a sweet one—opened, in my wordlessness, to the possibility of an uncomplicated kind of love.

After dinner, Hugo ran off to the kitchen. A few minutes later he reappeared, carrying a cake. As everyone clapped, he deposited it in front of me. It was buttercream, with a marzipan scroll that read, in English: "Welcome to Lauren."

THE NEXT MORNING, we slept late. When we woke, Olivier and I put on the bathrobes that Violeta had left out for us. Violeta and Teddy, in matching silk kimonos, were up, buzzing around the kitchen. They'd set up a table under a tree in the garden: silverware, cloth napkins, cheery red-and-white polka-dotted cups and saucers.

I was embarrassed.

"We slept until lunchtime?" I said to Olivier in English, drawing my bathrobe tighter around my waist.

He looked at me like I was confused.

"This is breakfast."

We all sat down, a phenomenon I was familiar with from cereal commercials. A plate of croissants went around, followed by jars of fig and strawberry preserves that Teddy had put up in the fall.

"Tea or coffee?" Teddy asked.

"Well, it's kind of weird," I began, "but I don't drink either."

I was waiting for Olivier to jump in and translate, but he remained silent.

"I don't know why—people always ask if I'm a Mormon, but nobody drank coffee in my family growing up, and I just never really got started," I babbled. "Actually, I'm not really big on any of the hot beverages, so I usually just drink water in the morning."

Olivier, finally coming to my aid, repeated my excuses—suspiciously, his rendition of the monologue took about half as long as the original version.

Violeta and Teddy looked at me with benign wonder, as though I'd said I didn't breathe air.

After breakfast, I went to take a shower. It was only after I'd stripped off all of my clothes that I realized that the toilet was in a separate room—an early lesson in the absolute demarcation between the scatological and the sensual, *les toilettes* and *la salle de bain*. There was one bathroom—of each type—for all of us. The latter was very much Violeta's domain. The ultimate sign of maturity, a friend of mine once claimed, is having a piece of furniture in your bathroom. This bathroom, with its framed nudes, frilled lampshades, and twin walnut bureaus, heaving with beads and eye shadows, spoke of a sort of deliberate, pleasure-taking womanhood that I wondered if I could ever claim.

A hand shower lurked in the corner, coiled around the faucet of an uncurtained bath. I stepped in, sat down, and slowly turned one of the taps to the left. A risky maneuver, I knew, freestyling with European plumbing, but I couldn't bring myself to call across the house for Olivier to help. Teddy was the kind of freakishly competent person who could rewire a lamp or explain how buttermilk was made. He washed rental cars. Violeta had grown up in a village in the Pyrenees. Even with four of us sharing a bathroom—later, it would be six, and eight—it never seemed to be occupied, Les Fockers slipping in and out like wraiths. I was clumsy in inverse proportion to their gracefulness. I had never felt so American, so conspicuous, so inured by comfort to common sense. Even the old-fashioned handles on the doors strained my technical skills. I could never open one of them—for example, to go to the bathroom in the middle of the night, which seemed like an opportune time—without it sounding like someone was popping balloons.

I loosened the tap a little further. It was the hot one, I soon found. The showerhead struck like a python, the hose writhing around the tub, firm as flesh, spraying searing water everywhere. Eventually I wrestled it into submission and turned off the tap.

Twisting my knees into lotus position, I quickly lathered my hair and turned the showerhead back on. Water trickled out, the python reduced to a caterpillar. Fearing that I was taking too long, I decided to forgo a rinse. I stepped out of the shower. Rolling my towel into a sponge, I got down on all fours and scrubbed the room dry, covered in suds and gooseflesh.

IN DECEMBER OF 1977, Jimmy Carter visited Poland, his first trip to a Communist country. He stepped off the plane, proceeded past an honor guard, and ascended a stage to deliver a speech that would be broadcast live on television. It was intended to be a human-rights landmark, a message of inspiration from the leader of the free world to the Polish people.

It was raining. For the occasion, the State Department, which did not have an interpreter on staff, had hired Steven Seymour, a respected translator of Russian, French, English, and Polish literature. ("Interpreter" and "translator" are often used interchangeably, but technically, an interpreter deals with speech, while a translator works with writing.) He was to be paid $150 a day. It was his first time interpreting for a head of state.

Carter opened the address with a nod to his hosts: "We are delighted to be in your great country. When I left the United States this morning, I told the people of my nation that this journey reflects the diversity of a rapidly changing world."

The State Department had not given Seymour, who was thirty-one, what is known in the trade as a Van Doren—a cram sheet named after Charles Van Doren, the contestant who was briefed in advance of his appearance on the quiz show *Twenty One*. Drenched and speaking in his fourth language, Seymour began to translate the president's words into Polish. Using the wrong conjugation of the verb "to leave," he accidentally implied that President Carter had permanently defected from America.

Oblivious to the gaffe, Carter went on, praising the Polish Constitution of 1791. Seymour somehow rendered it "an object of ridicule." Carter continued. "I have come not only to express our own views to the people of Poland but also to learn your opinions and to understand your desires for the future," he said. Choosing the wrong form of *desires*, Seymour announced to the nation that Carter was carnally desiring the Polish people.

Seymour was quickly relieved of his duties. For Carter's next engagement, a state banquet, the State Department brought on a Pole named Jerzy Krycki. When Carter stood up to deliver a toast, pausing after his first sentence so that the translator could relay his tribute, Krycki said nothing. Carter continued and paused again. Crickets. *Świerszcze.*

Krycki, it turned out, was experiencing the inverse of the

problem that plagued Seymour: he couldn't understand Carter's Georgia-inflected English. After the "carnal" fiasco, he had judged it wiser to simply remain silent. At last, one of the Polish officials' translators came to the rescue.

Interpreting emerged as a profession at the end of World War I, after President Woodrow Wilson and British prime minister Lloyd George insisted, in a break with precedent, that the Treaty of Versailles be negotiated and written in both French and English. (Since the Treaty of Rastatt, in 1714, French had enjoyed a monopoly as the language of high European diplomacy.) The Treaty of Versailles established the League of Nations. Its official languages were English, French, and Spanish, creating a permanent need for interpreters. At first, their techniques were limited to consecutive interpretation, in which the speaker stops periodically so that the interpreter can render his words into another language, and *chuchotage*, or "whispering translation," in which the interpreter sits or stands next to the listener and delivers a running commentary.

Chuchotage, clearly, was not going to work for the Nuremberg trials. And consecutive interpretation took so long that the proceedings would have gone on for years. The dilemma of convening the court in such a way that all of its participants—and, crucially, the world—could follow bedeviled its administrators. Robert H. Jackson, the chief US prosecutor at Nuremberg, wrote, "I think that there is no problem that has given me as much trouble and as much discouragement as this problem of trying to conduct a trial in four languages."

Eventually Jackson and his cohorts decided to take a gamble on a new method, simultaneous interpretation. At Nuremberg, twelve interpreters sat in the "aquarium"—four desks separated by low glass barriers—listening through headphones to the testimony, which they immediately rendered into English,

French, Russian, and German, transmitting each, through a microphone, to a dedicated radio channel. IBM had installed the cutting-edge system free of charge, "that all men may understand." Simultaneous interpretation requires almost superhuman neurological coordination. The task is so demanding that, at the United Nations, an interpreter typically works a shift of no more than twenty minutes.

The annals of diplomacy abound with incidents in which the garbled transmission of messages has had embarrassing, and even fatal, consequences. In July 1945, Allied leaders delivered the Potsdam Declaration to Japan, demanding an unconditional surrender. When reporters in Tokyo pressed Japanese premier Kantaro Suzuki for a response, he replied, using the word *mokusatsu*, that he was withholding comment. *Mokusatsu*—a portmanteau word, formed by combining the kanji characters for *killing* and *silence*—has several meanings: "to take no notice of; treat with silent contempt; ignore [by keeping silence]; remain in a wise and masterly inactivity." The press, however, took note only of its more belligerent connotations, and the world came to understand that the premier had deemed the Potsdam ultimatum "not worthy of comment." According to a report published years later in an NSA technical journal, "U.S. officials, angered by the tone of Suzuki's statement and obviously seeing it as another typical example of the fanatical Banzai and Kamikaze spirit, decided on stern measures." Even if *mokusatsu* was only one of many factors in the decision to drop the bomb, as was likely the case, it has lived on as a cautionary tale—history's "most tragic translation."

Eleven years later, at the height of enmity between the United States and the Soviet Union, Soviet premier Nikita Khrushchev delivered a speech in which he invoked the Russian phrase "Мы вас похороним." Idiomatically, the saying means something like "We'll be here even when you're gone," but Khrushchev's translator, Viktor Sukhodrev, relayed it literally as "We will bury you"—causing Americans to fear imminent nuclear war. (Sukhodrev said later that Khrushchev, with his fondness for hyperbole and folksy humor, was one of the most difficult people for whom to interpret.) Hillary Clinton returned the favor with her "reset" button of 2009. Intended as an emblem of her desire to improve US-Russian relations, it was emblazoned with the word *peregruzka*, which actually means "overcharged."

Mistranslation also wreaks havoc on individual fates. Particularly for immigrants attempting to navigate high-stakes institutions such as courts and hospitals, its consequences can be dire. Santiago Ventura Morales spent four years in prison for having murdered a fellow migrant worker on a strawberry farm in Oregon. Eventually his conviction was overturned—in part because he had gone through the entire trial with a Spanish interpreter, when in fact he spoke Mixtec.

In January 1980 Willie Ramirez, an eighteen-year-old Floridian, was taken by ambulance to the emergency room, having entered a coma after complaining of a headache that "felt like someone was sticking a needle through my head." He had pinpoint pupils and was breathing heavily. He was accompanied by his mother, his thirteen-year-old sister, his fifteen-year-old girlfriend, and his girlfriend's mother, all of whom believed that he had fallen ill after eating bad hamburger at a brand-new Wendy's.

Ramirez's mother didn't speak English, so his girlfriend's mother, who didn't speak English well, dealt with the doctors. "He is *intoxicado*," she said, using a Spanish term for any general kind of poisoning. The ER doctor later said, "Healthy, strapping kids don't come into the ER comatose unless they've been in a car accident or had an overdose. I thought my conversation with the family confirmed the diagnosis—that he had taken an overdose of drugs." It wasn't until nearly forty-eight hours later that someone, noticing that Ramirez had stopped moving his arms, called in a neurologist, who determined that Ramirez had actually suffered an intracerebellar hemorrhage. Due to the misdiagnosis, he became a quadriplegic. A jury awarded him damages of $71 million.

Translation implies a sense of movement—you translate something out of one language into another. The journey can be straightforward, a run to the dry cleaners, or it can be a grueling road trip across space and time. In mathematics, translation refers to "the movement of a body from one point of space to another such that every point of the body moves in the same direction and over the same distance without any rotation, reflection, and change in size." But in practice, translation often works more like a chemical reaction, in which one or more substances are converted into something else. The Chevy Nova is famously said to have sold poorly in Spanish-speaking countries, where *no va* means "doesn't go." The Nova actually did fine: the stresses in *Nova* and *no va* fall on different syllables, and Spanish speakers are as able to distinguish between them as English speakers are between *notable* and *not able*. But the history of marketing is full of linguistic flops. Sticking just with cars, Mitsubishi released a sports-utility vehicle called Pajero in Spain, where *pajero* means "masturbator."

Entrusting oneself to a translator, or to a translation, is an act of faith. A person who knows two languages can make fast fools out of those with only half his repertoire. In the mid-1990s Denis Duboule, a postdoctoral student in genetics in Strasbourg, France, came up with a new technique to produce duplications in the chromosomes of mice. Like 98 percent of scientists, he was to publish his findings in English. One Friday afternoon, he and some colleagues got together to decide what to call their discovery. Over beers, they hit upon TAMERE—"targeted meiotic recombination." In later papers, francophone researchers detailed their advances in sequential targeted recombination-induced genomic approach (STRING) and pangenomic translocation for heterologous enhancer reshuffling (PANTHERE). It wasn't until 2014 that English-speaking geneticists learned that their French-speaking peers, for the better part of two decades, had been having a laugh at their expense. *Ta mère* ("your mom") is shorthand for *niquer ta mère* ("fuck your mother"). The apotheosis of *mère*-slagging is *Ta mère en string panthère*—"Your mom in a leopard G-string."

The problem of translation is perhaps most acute in literature, to which renderings must be true in spirit as well as letter. Even the most diligent and creative translators find themselves hard-pressed to replicate such techniques as rhythm, assonance, alliteration, idiom, onomatopoeia, and double meaning. (Dr. Seuss books, with their oddball rhymes and invented words, are said to be the Nikita Khrushchevs of the written word.) Sometimes the loss is concrete: translators of *Harry Potter* found it impossible to convert the name Tom Marvolo Riddle—an anagram for "I am Lord Voldemort"—into many nonalphabetic East Asian languages, so they just left it out. Other times, it's ineffable but real. It is difficult to argue with Philip Larkin: "If that glass thing over there is a window, then it isn't a *fenster* or a *fenêtre* or whatever. '*Hautes Fenêtres*,' my God!"

Vladimir Nabokov spoke Russian, French, and English, all three more masterfully than the overwhelming majority of their respective constituencies. In 1951, when *Conclusive Evidence*, a memoir of his childhood in Russia, was published in

America, he confessed that he had found the task of rendering sensations that he had experienced in one language into another an anguish. "*Conclusive Evidence* was being written over a long period of time with particularly agonizing difficulties," he wrote, "because my memory was attuned to one musical key—the musically reticent Russian—but it was forced into another key, English and deliberate." It wasn't that Nabokov, as seamless a polyglot as there ever was, couldn't locate the English words; if they had existed, he would have known them. Rather, English seemed an improper vessel for his Russian memories. It was like trying to put water in a cardboard box.

Three years later, Nabokov translated *Conclusive Evidence* into Russian, producing *Drugie berega.* As the linguist Aneta Pavlenko notes in *The Bilingual Mind*, the book metamorphosed: "The translation for an audience of Russian émigrés made many explanations unnecessary, yet at the same time, the use of the childhood language triggered new memories, akin to the Proustian madeleine."

Both books contain detailed descriptions of Nabokov's family home at 47 Bolshaya Morskaya Street in St. Petersburg. Nabokov's first toilet, as he remembered it in *Conclusive Evidence*, was "casually situated in a narrow recess between a wicker hamper and the door leading to the nursery bathroom." The same room appears in *Drugie berega*, but this time with a sound track: "between a wicker hamper with a lid (how immediately I remember its creaking)!" There are new details: a stained glass window "with ornate designs of two halberdiers constructed from colorful rectangles"; a floating thermometer; a celluloid swan; a toy skiff. In 1966 Nabokov published *Speak, Memory*, a "re-Englishing of a Russian re-version of what had been an English re-telling of Russian memories in the first place." The thermometer vanished, but the halberdiers remained. Translation also has its gains.

If translation is a catalyst, the B that turns A to C, sometimes it seems to work in reverse. After translation, C does not revert to A, but rather into A+ (or A–), an entity that has been permanently altered by the transformation. "Dog days" sharpen their teeth as *canicules.* Bats (*les chauves-souris*) become bald mice. Learn French, and *umbrella* is, forever after, an overbroad concept: is it a *parapluie* (for rain) or a *parasol* (for sun)?

ON LABOR DAY—the French one, May 1—Violeta sent me an e-card decorated with a flashing lily-of-the-valley, enfranchising me into the global proletariat, and, I hoped, the family. My birthday came in June, accompanied by a necklace and a note, wishing me a happy day with my "love friend." Soon after, Olivier and I visited Andernos again. To win over the senior Madame Bovary, Emma endured rounds of dire conversation, "and even pushed deference to the point of asking her for a recipe for pickling gherkins." All I had to do was go on a bike ride to Le Truc Vert, a local beach. Splayed out on the sand, we made a funny pair—me in a T-shirt and sunscreen, and Violeta covered in oil, *seins nus*—but I admired her verve, her generosity, her sense of occasion, her femininity, at once steely and coquettish. I came from more pragmatic women. She was a different model, a space heater of a person, emitting warmth in extravagant blasts.

We were going to Andernos for Christmas that year. The holidays, in my parents' house, had always been an ambivalent time, coming, as they did, on the anniversary of John Zurn's death, and entailing two of my mother's least favorite things, cooking and the raising of expectations. Every year she grudgingly spent an afternoon in the kitchen, transforming Colman's mustard powder into gift jars of homemade mustard. My best friend Helen's mother, also named Sue, made mayonnaise. Per annual tradition, as soon as we stepped off the plane from New York, the respective Sues would send us out on overlapping delivery routes.

"I'm thinking of watching a foreign film this afternoon!" Sue No. 2 said one year, after a long day of condiment making.

"Which one?" Helen asked.

"It's called *Deuce Bigalow: European Gigolo.*"

On Christmas Eve we'd go all out, warming up a Honey-Baked Ham that one of my father's colleagues sent him every year, as a thank-you for referrals. My father drank Coors Original. My mother would have a glass of wine and then switch to Diet Coke. We'd long since stopped getting out the china, "since it's just the four of us." By the time the sun went down, we were usually in fleece. Often, we watched the hockey movie *Miracle*, chanting "U-S-A" as Mike Eruzione scored the game-winning goal.

In households across France, Christmas Eve was *le réveillon de Noël*—an elaborate feast meant to be served after Midnight Mass. We would not be going to church. (Olivier, having been baptized, called himself "a Catholic emeritus.") But I could see from the way the groceries were spilling out of the refrigerator that it was going to be a major affair. Olivier and I drove into Bordeaux to do some last-minute shopping. When we got back, I origamied myself into the bathtub and successfully washed my hair. Getting into the spirit, I put on a silky dress and doused myself with half a dozen more spritzes of Miss Dior Chérie than I'd usually wear.

Nine o'clock came and went. So did ten. Around ten thirty, the doorbell rang. Jacques, Marie, and Hugo came in, shaking off coats and scarves. They were carrying a trash bag full of presents. At some point Fabrice materialized, fresh off the plane from Paris. We all crowded into the living room, into which Teddy brought a lacquered tray that held a half dozen bowls—pistachios, cashews, potato chips, bugles, olives, cherry tomatoes—and a bottle of Champagne. He popped the cork and carefully poured eight flutes. *Réveillon* was under way.

To me, this was a storybook Christmas. There was jazz on the stereo. A fire crackled. I fancied myself at last at home among people who appreciated good food, good wine, the art of conversation. I didn't know what anyone was talking about, but I was content to occupy the role of armchair anthropologist.

My main research interests were how French people were able to remain so quiet in large groups and why, in multigenerational social settings, it was okay to step out for a cigarette (as Fabrice had just done) but not to ask for a refill of one's wine (in an attempt at pacing, I was making myself eat a cherry tomato before every sip). Eventually the finger food dwindled, and the rest of the group's glasses ran as dry as mine. At midnight, we toasted Hugo's birthday. There he was, a newly minted adolescent, stuck with a bunch of adults whose age surpassed his by a collective 317 years. He drank his Champagne slowly, made charming conversation without being precocious. I never saw his phone. Before every visit, Olivier and I said to each other, "Okay, he's totally going to be a brat this time." Every time he was delightful, playing James Blunt songs on the piano.

Teddy returned to the kitchen. A few minutes later, a tea party's worth of small cups appeared. They were filled with fanciful concoctions like salmon mousse, topped with chives that had been curled like ribbons. These were the cold appetizers. Hot ones followed: spring rolls, cod croquettes, skewers of chicken satay. It was almost one o'clock, and we were still on the snacks portion of the evening.

"À table!" Teddy said as the clock struck one thirty.

We sat down to a proliferation of gold and glass. Oysters came first, on plates of ice. Then slabs of foie gras the size of pieces of toast, surrounded by hillocks of salt. I was starting to feel like a human foie gras as Teddy emerged with stacks of blinis, glistening with caviar. He scurried back to the kitchen.

"Prost!" he said, the door swinging open. He was brandishing a platter of vodka shots—the *trou normand*, or "Norman hole," a mid-meal liquor break that was claimed to aid digestion.

Réveillon, it was becoming clear, was an endurance event. I had trained for a sprint. As *chapon farci aux fruits* blurred into *coquilles Saint-Jacques à l'ancienne*, I could barely keep my eyes open. Under the table, I kicked off my shoes, trying to jump-start my circulation. The night wore on. I kept pretending to sneeze so that I could turn away from the table, stealing glances at a digital clock that sat on the buffet. The red display barely seemed to budge. Two thirty-seven a.m.: salad. Two fifty-one: cheese course. I perked up momentarily when Violeta asked who wanted coffee, assuming that the offer was a euphemism for "Everybody go home."

"Oui!" Olivier responded.

"Moi!"

"Moi aussi!"

"Absolument!"

We packed back into the living room, where Teddy brought out a *bûche de Noël*, accompanied by another bottle of Champagne (and a mango ice cream cake for good measure). We ate the cake, we drank the wine. Several people had a second espresso. At last Violeta made an announcement: it was time to open presents.

CHRISTMAS—the house was as dead as a college dorm on a Sunday morning. Because breakfast, in a French family, cannot be skipped, we sat down at two and ate croissants and jam. This time I took some tea. Because lunch, in a French family, also cannot be skipped, even if you have just eaten breakfast, we returned to the table forty-five minutes later. Fortunately, lunch was soup.

It was a gray day, wood smoke choking the sky. We'd already stuffed our faces and torn through our presents: to an American, bred on hectic Christmas mornings, it felt a little anticlimactic. Jacques, Marie, and Hugo had dispersed. Fabrice had gone back to Paris. I suggested—well, sort of insisted—that the rest of us go to the movies, which was what my family always did on Christmas afternoon.

Violeta and Teddy kindly went along with it. We drove to the nearest multiplex, in Bordeaux. Our only criterion being that we needed something that everyone could understand, we decided to see *A Dangerous Method*, a historical film by David Cronenberg. It was playing in the original English version, with subtitles in French.

I was the only one to require popcorn. We proceeded into the theater and took our seats, close to the front: Teddy, me, Violeta, Olivier. The lights dimmed, and the curtains opened. Violins wailed as the screen filled with the opening credits.

The film began: a horse-drawn carriage barreling through verdant countryside while Keira Knightley, restrained by a pair of men in peaked caps, screams at the top of her lungs. The carriage arrives at a mansion on a hill, and the men join forces with a white-jacketed orderly to carry her, flailing, into the Burghölzli clinic near Zurich.

In the next scene, a door opens into a room with lots of molding.

"Good morning, I'm Dr. Jung," says a man with a mustache and a pocket watch. "I admitted you yesterday."

"I'm not . . . I'm not . . . *mad*, you know," Keira Knightley stutters in Eastern European–inflected English, jutting out her chin.

"Let me explain what I have in mind," Dr. Jung replies. "I propose that we meet here, most days, to talk, for an hour or two."

Soon Dr. Jung and Keira Knightley are enjoying a constitutional in a hardwood forest. When Keira Knightley drops her coat in the dirt, Dr. Jung picks it up and beats it with his cane. Keira Knightley makes an Edvard Munch face, soon confessing that any kind of humiliation makes her "so excited."

"Can you explain why your nights have been so bad?" Dr. Jung inquires during their next session.

She's afraid, she says. Just the night before, lying in bed, she experienced the sensation of a visitation by "something slimy, like some kind of mollusk moving against my back."

"Were you naked?" Dr. Jung wants to know. "Were you masturbating?"

Keira Knightley answers in the affirmative. All I could do, squeezed in between Teddy and Violeta, was to pray that the subtitler hadn't felt up to dealing with the shellfish.

Dr. Jung and Keira Knightley begin an affair. They ride steamboats in straw hats, sprawl out in the hull of a sloop, listen to arias. Eventually they consummate the relationship.

"Don't you think we ought to stop?" Dr. Jung asks.

YES!!! I screamed silently, staring straight ahead.

The camera cuts to Vienna: Jung and Freud, chomping on a cigar. They're sitting in Freud's study, droning on about catalytic exteriorization phenomena.

Relaxing, I went back to my popcorn. Then: a loud crackling sound made me bobble the bucket, sending kernels flying through the dark. I glanced up at the screen, where Dr. Jung was spanking Keira Knightley. She was bent over a brocade sofa, writhing like a fortune-telling fish.

I focused on the popcorn, chucking pieces into my mouth by the handful, crunching as loudly as I could in an attempt to override her moans.

At last we exited the theater. No one said a word. As we stepped out into the sodden Bordeaux night, I pulled up the hood of my coat, wanting to hide. After a few minutes, Violeta broke the silence.

"Quel beau film!" she said, grabbing my wrist. "*J'adore* Keira Knightley."

THE PROBLEM WITH THINKING of translation as a journey is that it's impossible to know where it starts. Just as science cannot tell us how or when human speech emerged in the grand scheme of human evolution, neither can it isolate the place, on the micro-scale, where instinct gives way to expression, biology shading into culture. Consider blinks and winks: a blink is an involuntary twitch of the eye; a wink is a conspiratorial signal. As the anthropologist Clifford Geertz pointed out, they are physiologically the same thing, contractions of the eyelid controlled by the orbicularis oculi muscle. An alien would not be able to distinguish between a guy with a mosquito in his face and one trying to pick her up at a bar. A French-speaking alien, for his part, would not know that *blink* and *wink* rhymed.

Darwin asserted that certain facial expressions are hard-wired, challenging the belief, dating from Aristotle, that the ability to smile and to laugh is a hallmark of civilization, distinguishing man from beast. At some point in history, Darwin wrote, facial expressions arose to serve evolutionary functions, and over the course of generations their association with emotion became ingrained. In 1972, to test Darwin's theory, the psychologist Paul Ekman asked subjects from a variety of backgrounds to look at photographs of facial expressions and to match them to a set of descriptive words. He identified seven basic universal emotions: happiness, sadness, anger, disgust, fear, surprise, and interest. These emotions, Ekman argued, manifest themselves in a corresponding set of facial expressions. In any corner of the world, happiness will entail "no distinctive brow-forehead appearance"; eyes that are "relaxed or neutral in appearance, or lower lids may be pushed up by lower face action, bagging the lower lids and causing eyes to be narrowed; with the latter, crow feet apparent, reaching from outer corner or eyes toward the hairline"; and, in the lower face, "outer corners of lips raised, usually also drawn back; may or may not have opening of lips and appearance of teeth."

Ekman is CEO of the Paul Ekman Group, which has worked with the CIA, the Department of Homeland Security, and the Department of Defense, along with Pixar and Google; he has written a book, *Emotional Awareness*, with the Dalai Lama. His Facial Action Coding System, "an anatomically based system for comprehensively describing all observable facial movement," breaks the range of human emotion down into forty-six Action Units ("neck tightener," "nostril compressor"), so that "practitioners who must penetrate deeply into interpersonal communications" (animators, law-enforcement officers) can read faces as though they were pictograms. To communicate while traveling abroad, he has claimed, you don't need a Berlitz book.

Before I met Olivier, I would have more or less agreed. People, it had always seemed to me, were more alike than they were different: they ate, they slept, they fought, they made up, they did their best for their children, they wanted to be loved. They didn't like to be too hot or too cold. They smiled when they were happy and cried when they were sad. Psychologists such as Ekman call the universal smile of true pleasure the Duchenne smile, after the French neurologist Guillaume Duchenne de Boulogne. By attaching electrodes to the faces of patients—the photographs have become a cult grotesquerie—he established that the smile that we perceive as joyful (versus smiles that mean all sorts of other things, from aggression to sarcasm) involved the activation of two groups of muscles: the zygomatic major (which controls the corners of the mouth) and the orbicularis oculi (the eyes).

If the Duchenne smile is the look, as Duchenne wrote, of "the sweet emotions of the soul," then Olivier, during the majority of our waking hours, did not appear to be having a very good time. I'd give him a compliment, and he'd remain impassive; we'd pose for a photo, and he'd stare straight ahead, as though it were a mugshot. His smile did not come nearly as often as I thought it should. When it did, it often struck me as half-watted, an energy-efficient flicker of the eyes.

Worse, his expression, at rest, seemed to me to constitute a snarl. He would assure me that nothing was wrong, but his knitted brows and pursed lips, overcast by five o'clock shadow, sent me into paroxysms of doubt. I was used to corn-fed faces, gentle chins and pinchable cheeks. The lack of softness in Olivier's look suggested to me a corresponding inner severity. I was forever coaxing him to show his teeth, which actually did annoy him. He seemed, on the other hand, to find my big American grin undignified. I was hurt by the way that, whenever we took pictures, he always deleted the ones in which I was mugging too uninhibitedly. I took it as some fundamental rejection of my character, of the ideals of fun and friendliness with which I had been brought up.

It is possible that faces are not as easily deciphered as Ekman and his disciples have suggested. Among other researchers, Lisa Feldman Barrett, who runs the Interdisciplinary Affective Science Laboratory at Northeastern University, in Boston, has disputed Ekman's methods. Suspecting that his preselected description words primed his subjects' responses, in the manner of leading polling questions, Barrett and her team conducted a similar set of experiments in which participants were not given any prompts. Their performance in describing faces plunged. When Barrett performed the tests upon a set of non-Western subjects—drawn from the Himba tribe of Namibia—she found that supposed distinctions between many facial expressions—for example, "happy" and "afraid"—fell apart. Barrett has written, "These findings strongly suggest that emotions are not universally recognized in facial expressions, challenging the theory, attributed to Charles Darwin, that facial movements might be evolved behaviors for expressing emotion." In other words: bring the Berlitz book.

In pre-Enlightenment Paris, the Duchenne smile was as rude as a sneeze or a fart. Since antiquity, experts on conduct had preached the advisability of a demure, closed expression.

Jesus wept. Ladies kept straight faces. Open orifices were for the rabble. "Greatness in kings," Richelieu advised, "resides in nothing offensive coming out of their mouths." Besides, almost everyone over forty, from paupers to princes, had appalling teeth. Those of the rich, who consumed the most sugar, were the worst. Louis XIV lost most of his jaw during a botched surgery for toothache; as a result, his physician wrote, "every time the king drank or gargled, the liquid came up through his nose, from where it issued forth like a fountain." To correct the defect, the king endured an operation in which a surgeon cauterized the perforation in his palate with an iron.

With the Enlightenment, the public display of emotion became acceptable. As revolutionary ideals spread in France, the open smile of the street seemed an attractive alternative to the tight-lipped court. In 1787 the Parisian dentist Nicolas Dubois de Chémant, dismayed by the smell of false teeth (they were made from hippopotamus ivory), invented porcelain dentures. Soon a smile was an accessory, as desirable an adornment as a powdered wig. "In late eighteenth-century Paris, the smile came to be viewed as symbol of an individual's innermost and most authentic self," Colin Jones writes in *The Smile Revolution*. "In a way that was perceived as both novel and modern, it was held to reveal the character of the person within." But the smile revolution, the expression of a time and place, was short-lived. "Face too jolly to be accounted a true republican," a guard at the Sainte-Pélagie prison commented, of one of the condemned.

Body language ceased to be a factor for us when, a year and a half after we'd met, Olivier moved to Geneva. The complications of long distance threw off our counterpoise: we'd get cut off on the phone and, five minutes later, still be trying to figure out where we had been. The old frustration of not being able to understand each other deepened with the new one of not being able to hear each other. A fight lurked in every dropped call. Needing all the cues we could get, we would attempt to Skype. The signal faded in and out, but even when it worked, it was a dispiriting exercise. Olivier had rented a small furnished apartment—a prefab bachelor pad—in the eaves of an old building. He was working long hours, and in the summer it got very hot. Day after day I clicked onto the same image: Olivier, eating spaghetti in his underwear, in front of a monstrous purple-and-green painting of Mick Jagger.

I still thrilled to London, but I was starting to wonder if it thrilled to me. Commuting across continents felt like a crime against not only the planet but also elementary human instincts. I feared I was becoming, without ever having wanted to, a member of some grim modern class that David Brooks would soon dub the aerostocracy: an estate of deracinated strivers, bullies of the boarding gate and hoarders of frequent-flyer miles, sealed off from anything that remotely resembled actual flourishing life on the ground.

This is a roundabout way of saying the thing that an educated, ambitious woman in the waning years of the first quarter of the twenty-first century is not supposed to say: I wanted very badly to get married. I had been conditioned for this, by where I came from and who I was. But the fact of being far away from my first sources of stability exacerbated my underlying biases to the point of fixation. My family was in North Carolina. My employer was in New York. My boyfriend was living in the Alps. Just the vocabulary of the situation felt like a mortification: Olivier was neither boy nor friend. (French, I would later learn, was even worse: if you weren't *mariée*, you were *célibataire*.) When a London friend asked, curious about the logistics of our setup, "Why are you still here?" the question reverberated like a metaphysical taunt.

I felt diffused: a place for nothing, and nothing in its place. All I could talk about was getting married, because all I could think about was getting married, which I was sure would give me the title—in the sense of a claim to some ground—that I craved. I saw marriage as almost a physical place, an island of safety. Olivier considered it a more vulnerable state. He told me, over and over again, that he loved me. He wanted to be together. He intended to have a family, and he intended to have it with me. But he was worried, he said, about the strains of being a bicultural couple, and he wanted us to take the time to be sure that we could manage a life stretched across two continents and two cultures. We needed to think about how we wanted to educate our children—whose sets of great-great-grandparents had all been born in different countries—and what would happen to them if something happened between us. We needed to figure out where we were going to live.

I had exactly two anxieties about cross-cultural marriage: (1) I feared being marooned, at the end of my life, in some French nursing home where no one had ever heard of baseball; and (2) it made me sad to think that my kids would miss out on one of the great joys of an American childhood, learning to spell *Mississippi*. But, generally, I didn't see what the big deal was. Tied up as I was in rules, timetables, and proverbs about buying cows, I couldn't take Olivier at his word.

Had Olivier been someone whose worldview I thoroughly understood—a God-fearing frat boy, say, from the American South—I would have been long and decisively gone. I could say with confidence that after thirty, the people whose minds I knew best asked the people they wanted to marry to marry them as soon as they knew that they were the people they wanted to marry. Most of my closest friends were married; the commitments, after they met the right people, had come fast. When I considered Olivier's friends—the majority of whom were in long-term relationships, many of them with children, but a minority of whom were technically wed—I didn't know whether I was taking into account a reasonable point of cultural contrast or deluding myself.

I was facing a problem of attribution, which prevented me from coming to credible conclusions, from which I could have taken confident action. I was perpetually unsure as to whether I was dealing with instances or patterns, individuals or groups, things or kinds. Trying to educate myself, I devoured books about French people, but they seemed farfetched, with their little black dresses and harmless affairs. They were really about a certain class of Parisians, no more applicable to Olivier and his family than an ethnology of wealthy Manhattanites would have been to mine. I didn't know whether Hugo was adorable because he was Hugo, or because French teenagers were well behaved. I couldn't tell whether Olivier's friends resisted marriage because they had different values than I did, or because people of their generation and background were uneasy about the relationship between their private lives, the church, and the state. There were too many variables. Did Olivier feel the way he did because (1) he was a guy; (2) he was French; (3) he was left-wing; (4) his parents had divorced; (5) he was scared of commitment; (6) he didn't love me enough; or (7) he was a left-wing French guy of divorced parents who was scared of committing because he didn't love me enough?

That year we went to my parents' house for Christmas, and then to Mexico, where we'd rented an apartment for a week.

The trip was tense. Deranged by our stalemate, I pushed in every direction, preferring any sort of movement to the status quo. I made passive-aggressive proposals of my own. I said we could get a civil partnership; I tried to gin up family pressure that didn't exist. All the while, I assured myself that Olivier was being manipulative, a wily European debaucher toying with the prospects of a straightforward American innocent.

The afternoon of New Year's Eve, we went snorkeling. Watching the angelfish swarm and scatter, I felt a momentary respite from months of disquiet, probably because I was physically forced to stop asking questions to which the answers would inevitably disappoint. The sea grass gesticulated; I was silent. That evening we drank margaritas and listened to a scruffy mariachi band in the town square. I said that I had to know now. We passed the saddest night trying to come to some sort of resolution. After the sun came up, we went for a walk.

"I just can't," Olivier said.

I called a taxi, decisive at last. At the airport, I ran up an enormous phone bill, speaking English to my American friends.

I boarded the plane. We sat on the runway for three hours before the pilot announced that our flight, the last of the day, was being canceled due to a mechanical glitch. Everyone disembarked. After great chaos, we were loaded into vans. I actually told the person sitting next to me that I was in transit to a family funeral, to justify my bursts of weeping. It was midnight before we arrived at a brightly lit tower complex. I spent the first night of the new year alone in a double bed on the twenty-first floor of an underbooked hotel on the Cancún strip.

Six days later, Olivier called. He was all in. The answer to why he felt the way he did, he explained, had been none of the above. I had been giving ultimatums to someone who preferred to come to his decisions in freedom.

I didn't know what to make of the situation. Violeta did, sending me a long e-mail with the subject line "Couple."

There, in my in-box, was the answer key, straight from his mother's mouth, to all the questions about Olivier that had harrowed me for years. I holed up for hours in front of my laptop, cutting and pasting phrases into Google Translate, consulting pronoun charts, trying to untangle prepositional phrases, checking the dictionary for shades of meaning, parsing tenses as though my future depended on it, which in a way it did. But reading the message was far beyond my abilities, and its content was too private to ask for help. I didn't know whether I was looking at a letter of recommendation or a death sentence.

So I zeroed in on what I could understand: "votre histoire d'amour," "vous êtes complémentaires sur tous les plans," "il t'aime." From what I gathered, this was positive. "Vous êtes faits l'un pour l'autre," Violeta had written. "You are made for one another." I decided to go with it.

Four

THE PRESENT

Le Présent

Bradley Cooper is the catalyst. I'm sitting at my desk one afternoon, surfing the Internet, when I come across a clip of him giving an interview on TF1, the French television channel. He's gargling his *r*'s like they're mouthwash. He even throws in a couple of *hein*s.

The interviewer asks how he learned French. He says that during college he spent six months living with a family in Aix-en-Provence. TF1 calls him "la coqueluche de Hollywood," using a word that has the unique distinction of being a homonym for *heartthrob* and *whooping cough.*

"Our viewers appreciate the fact that you spoke to us in French tonight," the interviewer says.

I click on another video, this one from an American channel called CelebTV.

"Who knew Bradley had this secret weapon for getting the ladies? He's totally fluent in French!"

Like the presenter, I'm impressed. An excellent command of French seems like a superpower, the prerogative of socialites and statesmen. The prerequisite for speaking French, I have always thought, is being the kind of person who speaks French.

I need French like a bike messenger needs a bicycle. I consider myself a fish. One day I see a woman named Alessandra Sublet on television and pronounce her name "sublet," like what you do to an apartment, achieving a sort of reverse Tarzjhay effect. But there's Bradley Cooper, nailing his uvular fricatives on the evening news. I tell myself the same thing I do when faced with such challenges as doing my taxes: if that guy can hack it, I can too. Maybe you don't speak French because you're privileged; you're privileged because you speak French. The language suddenly seems mine for the taking, a practical skill. Herbert Hoover was fluent in Mandarin.

On a blustery morning in mid-March, I report for my first day of school. The class I've signed up for is being held at the Service Culturel Migros Genève headquarters, which occupies a big limestone building just off rue du Rhône, Geneva's main drag. While technically Switzerland's largest supermarket chain—the one with no booze and the Hitler coffee creamers—Migros has also cornered the market in the instruction of such disciplines as jewelry design, ikebana, equitation, Bollyrobics, and foreign language. On the last count, the fact that the school's body-conditioning course is called "Good Morning Wonderbras" does not inspire tremendous confidence.

The entryway is shaded by a metal canopy, which bears a pistachio-colored neon sign in the sort of fusty font that a New York restaurateur would die for. Inside, a canteen offers hot meals, eaten on damp trays. Sleepy-eyed students take their coffee at tables of teal linoleum. Smoking is no longer allowed, but its accretions remain, adding to the sensation of having enrolled in a Laundromat in 1970.

I climb the stairs to room 401. We're a dozen or so, sitting at four tables arranged in a rectangle. For the next month, we will meet five hours a day. The professor introduces herself. She is Swiss, in her sixties, with leopard-print bifocals and a banana clip.

"I am Dominique. Just call me Dominique. Not *Madame*—Dominique. I will *tutoyer* you. You can *tutoyer* me, too," she says, indicating that we're all to use the informal form of address. "I'm from Lausanne."

Lausanne, by train, is thirty-three minutes from Geneva.

"The *genevois*," she adds, "consider the *lausannois* very provincial."

THE CLASS IS INTENSIVE French B1—a level into which I've placed after taking an online test. According to the diagnostic, I can get by in everyday situations, but I can't explain myself spontaneously and clearly on a great number of subjects. This is true: like a soap opera amnesiac, I'm at a loss to articulate things of which I do not have direct experience. Still, I'm pleased that after eight months in Geneva, my piecemeal efforts at picking up the language, which consist mostly of reading free newspapers, have promoted me from the basest ranks of ignorance. One day, when the front-page headline reads "Une task force pour contrôler les marrons chauds," I grasp that Geneva is about to sic the police on the vendors of hot chestnuts.

Language, in delineating a boundary that can be transgressed, is full of romantic potential. Supposedly, the best way to master a foreign language is to fall in love with a native speaker. For the philosopher Emmanuel Levinas, the erotic intention amounted to a "sublime hunger" for the other, the more foreign the more delectating. It is no accident that the metonym for language is a tongue, not an ear, an eye, or a prehensile thumb. A willingness to take one on—to take one *in*, filling one's mouth with another's words—suggests pliancy, openness to seduction. It worked for Catherine of Valois (Henry V, English), and Jane Fonda (Roger Vadim, French). One can only hope that one day the hardworking farm boy from Rosetta Stone dazzles the Italian supermodel with his command of the *congiuntivo trapassato.*

Lust can be an accelerant to learning, feeding flares of insight. Scholars of Flaubert dream of recovering the manuscript of *Madame Bovary* that he mentioned in an 1857 letter to his Parisian publisher: "An English translation which *fully* satisfies me is being made under my eyes. If one is going to appear in England, I want it to be this one and not any other one." The translator was Juliet Herbert, an Englishwoman who had come to the family estate at Croisset—Flaubert's riverine sanctuary of honeysuckle twining iron balustrades—to serve as governess to Flaubert's niece. At night, she instructed Flaubert in English. "I am still doing English with the governess (who excites me immeasurably; I hold myself back on the stairs so as not to grab her behind)," he wrote to a friend. "If I go on, in six months I will read Shakespeare as an open book." The translation that they made together is as lost as a love letter. Imagine, if it were wrought with such care and tenderness, what perfect correspondence they may have attained.

The sublime hunger may have gnawed at even as doughty a character as Queen Victoria. At the age of seventy she took up Urdu, promoting Abdul Karim, a twenty-four-year-old table servant—he had been a gift from India upon her Golden Jubilee—to the role of *munshi*, or private tutor. Each afternoon, the pair met to practice the language. As Shrabani Basu writes in *Victoria & Abdul*, "Karim would write a line in Urdu, followed by a line in English and then a line of Urdu in roman script."

In the final years of her life, Karim became Victoria's closest confidant. She built a cottage for him at Balmoral and tried to have him knighted, to the dismay of her entourage. She rebuked Lord Elgin, the viceroy of India, for failing to acknowledge a Christmas card that he had sent. "Young Abdul (who is in fact *no* servant) teaches me and is a vy. strict Master, and a *perfect* Gentleman," she wrote to one of her daughters in 1888. It's impossible to know the exact nature of their relationship, as less than a week after Victoria's death, her son King Edward ordered their letters burned. Over the course of the years, Victoria had filled thirteen red-and-gold copybooks:

You may go home if you like	*Tum ghar jao agar chhate ho*
You will miss the Munshi very much	*Tum Munshi ko bahut yad karoge*
The tea is always bad at Osborne	*Chah Osborne men hamesha kharab hai*
The egg is not boiled enough	*Anda thik ubla nahi hai*
Hold me tight	*Ham ko mazbut Thamo*

LOVE IS THE CAUSE and the continuance of my commitment to learning French, its tinder and its fuelwood, but, pedagogically, I'm having less success with the soul mate method. Olivier does not materialize at the tinkle of a handbell, attired in turban and sash, nor does he proofread my letters, blotting my mistakes with light pink paper. More prosaically, he is completely deaf in his right ear (meningitis, when he was three). He's freakishly adept at keeping up with conversation—even in his second language, at a 50 percent disadvantage—but in order to hear, he has to turn his head so that he's looking almost directly over his right shoulder, which forces him to speak out of the far left corner of his mouth, as though he's perpetually telling a dirty joke. Enunciation is not his strong suit. His syntax can be equally askance. He starts sentences and lets them trail off, circling back after he's put whatever he was going to say through another lap of thought.

We don't speak French as regularly as we should. We try, but it's hard, with English at our disposal, to summon the willpower to dial back to a frequency devoid of complexity, color, and jokes. Had my language skills developed in tandem with our relationship—the ability to say things mirroring my desire to say them—we might have gotten into the habit. But the moment for languid afternoons, naming the knees and the eyelashes, has passed. Our classroom is the kitchen after a long day, extractor fan howling. Olivier's uptight (he can't let an error go without correcting it). I'm impatient (the moment I make one, I abandon the effort). We can't seem to lower our inhibitions and just let the conversation flow, the way you're supposed to do to enter another language. When I try out a new word, I feel conspicuous, as though I'm test-driving a car I can't afford. It's hard for me, as someone for whom English is a livelihood, to embrace my status as an amateur in French. I'm the opposite of Eliza Doolittle: I don't want to speak like a lady in a flower shop, I want to speak grammar.

Sybille Bedford captured the stylized pugnacity with which the French often confront foreigners, describing the pattern of "a great verbal roughing up at the beginning followed by showers of charm and goodwill; one might nearly get thrown out for expecting a table then end up dinner with brandy on the house." The Swiss, however, make no such fetish of banter. Theoretically, I'm living in an immersion environment, but even outside the house, my exposure to French is limited. I feel as ridiculous about this as I would if I had moved to Europe and found myself eating a cheeseburger every day for lunch. I always begin in French when I enter a store, sit down in a restaurant, ask whether a seat's taken on the tram. But language isn't the totem of pride and identity in Switzerland that it is in France. It's an instrument. Three times out of four, my interlocutor, hearing my accent, answers in English.

The solution seems obvious: push on in French. But the situation is tricky. My neighbors are essentially offering me cheeseburgers, prepared at some expense, and to turn them down seems unappreciative. Speaking English is a status symbol. It can also be a form of one-upmanship, a gauntlet being laid. "I've paid my dues in English," I feel I'm being told, "now don't waste my time with your rickety French."

On Wednesdays I meet with a conversation partner for a language exchange: an hour of English for an hour of French. I'm hurrying to the café, trying to take in every billboard and notice and poster—the street's own flash cards, shuffling by—when I pass a restaurant with a large, expensive-looking slate affixed to its facade:

IN HAMBURGER WE TRUST.
BECAUSE WE LIKE IT.
WHEN IT'S HURT HARD.

I double back, pausing on the sidewalk in front of the building. That's really what it says.

Mistranslations are supposed to be funny, the stuff of bathroom books and Internet memes. But I'm blindsided by rage—a territorial desire to inflict upon whoever wrote this gibberish the shame, the self-conscious constraint, that I experience in his language every day. I want one person, one time, to know that you can't explain someone something, to say *furniture* without putting an *s* on the end, to use *funny* to mean "humorous." Geneva feels like a reverse Babel, with everyone, from everywhere, speaking a common language—*my* language—poorly. International English is beginning to be my *bête noire*, which I'd probably call "beast black" if I were speaking International English.

Half seriously, I fantasize about going through my days pretending to be Russian—"Nyet," I'd say, and steamroll my way through the doctor's appointment *en français*—thinking how much faster I'd progress. French is a secret garden, but English, somehow, is everyone's property. While I was gone, strangers have moved into my childhood home, ripped down the curtains, and put their feet up on the couch.

"ALORS!" Dominique says.

For our first classroom assignment, we're to conduct a conversation with the person next to us, and then introduce him or her to the group. We spend the next ten minutes chatting haltingly—an awkward silence passes over the crowd roughly every twenty seconds—before Dominique calls the class to attention.

"Lauren, you will be my first victim!"

A hacky sack, confirming that I have the floor, comes sailing across the room.

"Je vous présente Lana," I begin.

Lana, a twenty-six-year-old Bosnian Serb, likes gymnastics. She comes from Banja Luka, a town with a temperate climate, several discotheques, and a thirteenth-century fort. Lana is in Geneva with her husband, who works at a bank. She doesn't mention a job, but she looks like a salon model, with crimson fingernails and thick brown hair, plaited like a dressage contestant. She is the second of three sisters. She takes copious notes with a mechanical pencil that she produces from a plastic case. When she makes a mistake, she scrubs at it with a gum eraser, delicately blowing the leavings, as though she were wishing on a dandelion, from the page.

It's Lana's turn to introduce me.

"Je vous présente Lauren."

Lana explains that I come from a village in North Carolina. I like books and traveling. Lana does an impeccable job, except that she says *magasin américain* instead of *magazine américain*, so everyone thinks I work in an American store instead of for an American magazine. "Freedom isn't free!" I imagine myself admonishing shoppers who question the markups on peanut butter and flag pins.

A nice thing about Geneva: the city offers an annual *chèque de formation* in the amount of 990 Swiss francs to anyone who cares to claim it. So the class, which costs exactly 990 Swiss francs, is populated by a group of citizens who, for one reason or another, want—*need*—to learn French in a less dilatory way than that of your typical adult-education enthusiast. No one is here to check off his bucket list or to prepare for a holiday abroad. The fantasy of the foreigner is a life more banal.

Sonia, a young Galician who delivers newspapers, introduces Jorge, a single Argentinian architect in his forties.

"His hobbies are playing soccer and watching soccer."

"What else do you like, besides soccer?" Dominique asks.

"Cooking—my mother's dishes," he responds, reddening from stubbly neck to chubby cheeks. He seems to think that Dominique is hitting on him.

We meet Nino, a bank intern from Lucerne; Claudia, a Bolivian home health-care aide; Carlos, a Spanish bellboy; a Japanese academic named Satomi; and three young Italian women—Cristina, an artist; Giulia, who has followed her husband to Geneva; and Alessandra, who has come with her boyfriend. The only other American in the class is Scotty, an executive at an NGO. She comes from Alaska, which, she announces, is "not really part of the United States."

Frank, a married German who works in development and likes running, clears his throat and launches into an introduction of the student to his left, in a baseball cap and hooded sweatshirt.

"Vic est canadien," he says.

"Canadien ou canadienne?" Dominique interrupts, assuming Frank has made a rookie mistake in gender agreement.

Next door, the Bollyrobics class is blasting bhangra. Frank starts again.

"Il est canadien."

The room falls silent as Frank turns to reassess his partner.

"Elle est canadienne," he says, recovering quickly. "Elle

aime bien le rugby. Elle est un chef de cuisine. Sa spécialité est poisson."

THE FIRST WORDS we have in what can be called French troth a fratricide. The year is 842: Louis the German and Charles the Bald, grandsons of Charlemagne, are under attack from their eldest brother Lothair, who, as the nominal head of the Frankish Empire, is burning, pillaging, and murdering people in their territories. Louis controls East Francia, which aligns with much of modern-day Germany. Charles rules West Francia, covering parts of what is now France. (The word *Francia* refers to the Franks, the Germanic tribe that established the Frankish Empire.) With their armies, they convene at Strasbourg, pledging to unite against Lothair.

The historian Nithard, also a grandson of Charlemagne, chronicled their accord in *On the Dissensions of the Sons of Louis the Pious*, a sort of grisly family newsletter. According to him, Louis speaks first, addressing his troops in Frankish, an early form of German. "Let it be known how many times Lothair has—since our father died—attempted to destroy me and this brother of mine, committing massacres in his pursuit of us," he says. "But since neither brotherhood nor Christianity nor any natural inclination, save justice, has been able to bring peace between us, we have been forced to take the matter to the judgement of almighty God." Charles follows, making a similar speech in Gallo-Romance, a prototypical French. Finally the brothers swear an oath, each reciting it in the other's language—the ultimate way of signaling their good intentions. (They read aloud from phonetic texts.) "With this completed," Nithard writes, "Louis left for Worms along the Rhine via Speyer; and Charles, along the Vosges via Wissembourg."

The Oaths of Strasbourg were kind of like our wedding, at which various participants, in order to bond with the other side of the family, chose to address the crowd in languages of which they did not have an entirely sturdy grasp. Jacques stood up and talked about "a very nice American movie, *Love Story*." My friend Helen, in from Wilmington, kicked off with a four-syllable "Bienvenue." Olivier alternated between French and English. So did I, having sent off my speech to a translator I found on the Internet. Fortunately, he was more conscientious than the celebrant who, in the Maldives in 2010, led a Swiss couple in a renewal of their vows. "You fornicate and make a lot of children," he said in the Dhivehi language as the couple looked on, clasping hands. "You drink and you eat pork. Most of the children that you have are marked with spots and blemishes. These children that you have are bastards."

Both Frankish and Gallo-Romance were members of the Indo-European language group, meaning that—among some five hundred languages, including English, Spanish, Russian, Sanskrit, and Hindi—they are thought to share a common ancestor, which likely emerged in Eastern Europe and Central Asia somewhere around 3500 BC. Frankish was part of the Germanic branch. (So is English.) Gallo-Romance, on the other hand, derived from Latin, which had dominated the lands that would eventually be France since 50 BC, when the Romans had conquered the Celts.

The meeting was extraordinary, not for what the brothers said, but for the fact that it was recorded in the manner in which they said it. Most contemporary documents of any importance were written in Latin, but the scribes at Strasbourg chose to render the day's events verbatim. The Oaths of Strasbourg thus constitute the first written example of what will eventually become modern French. The next year the Treaty of Verdun dismantled the Carolingian Empire, dividing the continent among the three brothers from the Atlantic to the Rhine. Monique Fuchs, of the Strasbourg Historical Museum, has written, "Thus began the history of the peoples of Europe, each identifying itself with a specific language and political organization."

French, at the turn of the first millennium, was coming into its own. Its influences were various. Gaulish, the language spoken by the Celts, had surrendered to vulgar Latin five hundred years earlier, but its traces persisted, most palpably in the vocabulary of botany and agriculture: *alouette* (lark), from *alauda*; *chêne* (oak), from *cassanos*; *mouton* (sheep), from *multo*. In the late fifth century, the Western Roman Empire fell to German invaders. They failed to impose their languages on the continent, but they left their mark in words such as *gant* (glove) and *guerre* (war). Their presence accelerated the fragmentation of colloquial Latin. As the empire splintered, so did its patterns of speech, giving rise to a rustic spin-off of Latin called Romance. Speakers of Romance dropped the inflected cases of Latin, reducing them to the nominative (subject) and the accusative (object). To indicate gender and number, articles multiplied.

Romance itself spawned subcategories, which became the Romance languages. By 1000, Spanish, Italian, Portuguese, Romanian, and French were being spoken in recognizable but unstable forms. In the thirteenth century twenty-two varieties of Romance—Angevin, Auvergnat, Berrichon, Bourbonnais, Bourguignon, Champenois, Croissant, Français, Franc-Comtois, Gallo, Gascon, Languedocien, Limousin, Lorrain Roman, Norman, Orléanais, Picard, Poitevin, Provençal, Saintongeais, Tourangeau, Walloon—existed in France alone. Français—the dialect of the Île-de-France region, encompassing Paris—

would eventually elbow out the others, claiming the title of what we now know as French.

In 1539 François I issued the Ordinance of Villers-Cotterêts, requiring that all official documents be written in "the French mother tongue and not otherwise." The decree institutionalized a reality that had been emerging for several centuries: for pretty much everyone but the priests, Latin was dead. The Académie Française—the world's first national body dedicated to the stewardship of a language—was established in 1635, "to give certain rules to our language and to render it pure, eloquent, and capable of treating the arts and sciences." Competing with the Italian states throughout the Renaissance, France pursued *rayonnement*—literally, "radiation," but more generally, standing—via French, its most glorious tool of public relations. The state's linguistic chauvinism justified itself elegantly: so many amazing things were produced in French that it stood to reason that French produced amazing things. In 1782, much of the European elite would have agreed with Antoine de Rivarol, who wrote, "If it's not clear, it's not French."

"MON CONJOINT, MON CONJOINT, mon conjoint," I whisper to myself as the tram inches past medical-equipment emporia and a hundred men wearing the same thinly striped cashmere scarf. "Mon conjoint, mon conjoint, mon conjoint, mon conjoint, mon conjoint, mon conjoint, mon conjoint, mon conjoint, mon conjoint, mon conjoint, mon conjoint, mon conjoint, mon conjoint, mon conjoint."

Dominique has a theory, not scientifically proven, that to memorize a word you have to say it seventeen times. I start at the top of the worksheet she's given us about the family. *Mon conjoint*: "my spouse." I wonder why the compiler of the list has chosen to leave out the direct cognate, *époux*, as well as *mari/femme*, the words I've heard more often for husband and wife. *Conjoint* sounds like an army rank, or something you would say at a convention, while wearing a lanyard: "Jerry, shake hands with my *conjoint*."

My vocabulary is improving. The dictionary app that I use allows you to track the words you've looked up. It reads like a diary, a logbook of my days:

shelf	planche
frustrated	agacé
cote	quotation
côte	slope
coté	sought-after
côte-a-côte	side by side
côté	side
coter	to price
courriel	mail
lettre	letter
require	exiger
racheter	to buy some more
scissors	ciseaux
aspire	aspirer
squash	potimarron
soupière	tureen
rêve	dream

I treasure each acquisition, remembering the exact circumstances—time, place, company—under which it was made. English is a trust fund, an unearned inheritance, but I've worked for every bit of French I've banked. In French, words have tastes and textures. They come in colors and smells. *Ruban* is scarlet and scratchy, the stuff we bought before a costume party to tie a letter *A* around my neck. *Hirondelle* will always be an easy hike on a gray day in May. We're ticking off the stations of the cross, which a Savoyard devout has installed on a rocky slope side. We're scampering up it, Olivier becoming the first man to ascend a pre-Alp while carrying a golf umbrella. "Une hirondelle ne fait pas le printemps"—One swallow doesn't make spring—he says, citing a typically gloomy French proverb. The sky rips open as we reach Calvary.

I continue down the list. There's a section for *la famille recomposée*, the blended family. The prefix seems a two-letter proof of the French insistence on history versus the American faith in fresh starts. (I later learn that the French, amazingly, call life insurance "death insurance.") The inclusion of *Ramadan* strikes me as the equivalent of putting *quinceañera* in an English book, but at least it's a gimme. *La belle-mère* is a lovely phrase. I fail to understand, though, how it can simultaneously mean "mother-in-law" and "stepmother." Even homonymically, does anyone want her husband's mom to be the same woman who married her father?

I finish chanting the sixteen members of the close, extended, and blended families and proceed to the first written exercise. "The relations between members of the family are sometimes complex," it asks. "What unites them or divides them most often?" The worksheet gives five choices: respect, trust, complicity, jealousy, and rivalry. You're supposed to match them with prompts—"The brothers and sisters ______," "The mother and her daughter ______," "The father and his daughter ______"—like some kind of Freudian Mad Libs.

"Open your books to page nineteen," Dominique says when class begins.

The textbook is *Latitudes 3*, by Y. Loiseau, M.-N. Cocton, M. Landier, and A. Dintilhac. I skim the table of contents. Chapters 9 and 4, respectively, are entitled "Green and Against It All!" and "Are You Zen?" *Mon conjoint*, the eighteenth time around, starts to make more sense.

"Today," Dominique says, "we are going to make a time capsule."

We divide into groups. I'm with Jorge, the Argentinian architect, and Claudia, from Bolivia.

"What is the most important event of the past twenty years?" I ask, reading aloud from the lesson. (The time capsule is to consist of our thoughts.)

"Pope Francis!" Jorge says.

Claudia and I exchange a look.

"Or the Internet?" she ventures.

Claudia and Jorge begin debating the events of 1994–2014 in a sort of unfollowable Sprench. I remember that I hate working in groups. Technically, we're all speaking French, but each national faction mangles the language uniquely, as though we're a bunch of convalescents, each with a different injury, trying to partner up for a ballroom dance. The paradox of foreign language classes is that they isolate you with perfect precision from the population of which you're attempting to become a part. A French class is, by definition, the one place where you're never going to find a person who speaks French.

Eventually I jump in.

"Definitely the Internet."

Jorge really wants to talk about the pope.

"Corruption is everywhere in Argentina," he says, in English. "But Francis is a good man."

"D'accord," I say, giving up.

Dominique clears her throat and asks which group would like to share its conclusions. No one volunteers.

"Spring," she says, gazing at snowdrifts melting on the eaves outside. "Emotionally, it's not always easy."

She decides that we'll go around the room.

"What personalities have made the biggest contribution to the world?"

"Mandela, Obama, and Jobs."

"What food product have you discovered for the first time in the past twenty years?"

"Foie gras, sushi, and goji berries."

Before dismissing class, Dominique suggests that, as a learning aid, we paper our apartments with Post-it Notes, each listing the French name of the object on which it's stuck.

"Be creative!" she says.

Before the end of the term, she announces, we'll each be expected to give an oral presentation.

"It's a test, yes, but also a psychological experience."

DESPITE ITS PRETENSIONS TO CLARITY, French can be trying. *Vert* (green), *verre* (glass), *ver* (worm), *vers* (toward), and *vair* (squirrel fur) constitute a quintuple homonym, not even counting *verts*, *verres*, and *vers* (you don't pronounce the final *s* in French). Folklorists have argued for decades over whether Cinderella's *pantoufle en verre* might have come about as a mishearing, on Charles Perrault's part, of *pantoufle en vair.* The subjunctive is a wish. Gender's a bitch. *Le poêle*: a stove. *La poêle*: a frying pan. A man's shirt, *une chemise*, is feminine, but a woman's shirt, *un chemisier*, is masculine. Imagine everyone you've ever met looking exactly alike, and then, four decades into your acquaintanceship, having to go back and try to figure out who's a man and who's a woman. And then, to make matters more complicated, some of the men are women and some of the women are men.

French isn't actually exceptionally difficult. In fact, it is becoming ever easier, as large languages are wont to do: one linguist found that every verb created since 1950 uses the regular -*er* ending, making it easy to figure out that the past participle of *zlataner*—to dominate, like the football player Zlatan Ibrahimović—is *zlatané*. The Malian language Supyire has five genders (humans, big things, small things, groups, liquids), while the Australian language Ngan'gityemerri has fifteen (males, females, groups, animals, vegetables, body parts, canines, trees, liquids, fire, strikers, digging sticks, woomeras, two different types of spears).

It is a truism of linguistics that every language is equally complex. This is true in that every language is complex—"When it comes to linguistic form, Plato walks with the Macedonian swineherd, Confucius with the head-hunting savage of Assam," the linguist Edward Sapir wrote in 1921—and in that no language is any harder or easier for a native speaker to acquire. The !Xóõ language of Botswana has a hundred and twenty-five consonants (including seventy-eight clicks), but no !Xóõ-speaking child grows up thinking that !Xóõ is too hard to learn. For non-native speakers, though, some languages clearly present more of a challenge than others. Which ones those are depends on the language with which you begin. A colleague who grew up speaking Mandarin moved to America when she was eight. She recalls feeling exasperated in her middle-school French class: "Most of the vocabulary sounded similar, and as someone who had just struggled to adjust to English, I couldn't believe that French wasn't regarded as just another dialect of

English." For her, English was a vexing thing to speak aloud. As Charles Ollier pointed out, *fish* might well be spelled *ghoti* (*gh* as in *tough*, *o* as in *women*, *ti* as in *mention*). Recently, the Facebook page of the European Commission's interpreters featured a post entitled "This is why we love (and hate) the English language!" It included a poem called "The Chaos," by the late Dutch anglophile Gerard Nolst Trenité:

> Dearest creature in creation,
> Study English pronunciation.
> I will teach you in my verse
> Sounds like corpse, corps, horse, and worse.
> I will keep you, Suzy, busy,
> Make your head with heat grow dizzy.
> Tear in eye, your dress will tear.
> So shall I! Oh hear my prayer.
> Pray, console your loving poet,
> Make my dress look new, dear, sew it!

The poem went on for 104 more lines.

Linguists have attempted to make an objective assessment of the relative difficulty of languages by breaking them down into parts. One factor is the level of inflection, or the amount of information that a language carries on a single word. The languages of large, literate societies have larger vocabularies. One might think that their structures are also more elaborate, but the opposite is true: the simpler the society, the more baroque its morphology. In Archi, a language spoken in the village of Archib in southern Dagestan, a single verb—taking into account prefixes and suffixes and other modifications—can occur in 1,502,839 different forms. This makes sense if you think about it. Because large societies have frequent interaction with outsiders, their languages undergo simplification. Members of relatively homogeneous groups, on the other hand, share a base of common knowledge, enabling them to pile on declensions without confusing each other. Small languages stay spiky. But, amid waves of contact, large languages lose their sharp edges, becoming beveled as pieces of glass.

Another way to try to rate the difficulty of languages is to consider their unusual features: putting the verb before the subject in a sentence, for example, or not having a question particle. Coders analyzed 1,694 languages for twenty-one semantic quirks to create the Language Weirdness Index, anointing Chalcatongo Mixtec—a verb-initial tonal language spoken by six thousand people in Oaxaca—the world's hardest language. The most straightforward was Hindi, with only a single unusual feature, predicative possession. English came in thirty-third, making it a third as weird as German, but seven times weirder than Purépecha.

According to the US State Department, French is among the easiest languages for an English speaker to learn. It requires an estimated six hundred hours of instruction, versus eleven hundred for Pashto or Xhosa and twenty-two hundred for Arabic or Mandarin. Thanks to the Normans, who invaded England in the eleventh century, somewhere between a quarter and half of the basic English vocabulary comes from French. Modern-day English speakers, in fact, are able to read Old French more easily than their French counterparts, due to the persistence of forms of words that have disappeared from the latter language: *acointance*, *plege*. An English speaker who has never set foot in a bistro already knows an estimated fifteen thousand words of French.

The challenge, I'm finding, is figuring out which ones. Is *challenge*, for example, something else entirely in French, or just a matter of Coopering out a "shal-longe"? Certainly a native English speaker has an easier time in French than one of Mandarin, but the availability of cognates can lull him into a false sense of security, a tendency to imagine he's making himself clear when he's not. He doesn't know what he doesn't know. His misplaced confidence throws his interlocutor, who might take more care with someone he recognized to be blatantly out of his depth. As much as I felt for my colleague, having to conjure French out of nothing, I envied her the purity of the blank slate.

French is not a hospitable environment in which to try your luck. The thing that's tough about French is the thing that's exemplary about French, which is that French speakers across the board are language nuts. Jean-Benoît Nadeau and Julie Barlow write, "Debates about grammar rules and acceptable vocabulary are part of the intellectual landscape and a regular topic of small talk among francophones of all classes and origins—a bit like movies in Anglo-American culture."

American politicians play golf or sing in barbershop quartets; French statesmen—who cultivate a sort of spiritual innumeracy in contrast to the spiritual illiteracy of their American counterparts—moonlight as men of letters. (Charles de Gaulle was famous for resurrecting obscure bits of vocabulary.) It took Olivier three weeks and a working group of twice as many relatives to settle on the French text of our wedding invitation, which read, in its entirety, "Together with our families, we request the pleasure of your company at a wedding lunch." The ideas of excellence and failure are so intimately linked in French that what passes for a compliment is to say that someone has *un français châtié*—a well-punished French. Olivier has fond memories of watching the grammarian Bernard Pivot, a national celebrity, administer the *Dicos d'or*, a live televised tournament—the Super Bowl of orthography—in which contestants vied to transcribe most flawlessly a dictated text.

Pivot's competition was inspired by the *dictée de* Mérimée, a moment in French history to which you will find no English analogue. On a rainy day in 1857 at Fontainebleau, the royal country estate, Empress Eugénie asked the author Prosper Mérimée to concoct an entertainment. Mérimée gathered the party. He handed out pens and paper, instructing the guests to jot down the composition he was about to read: "Pour parler sans ambiguïté, ce dîner à Sainte-Adresse, près du Havre, malgré les effluves embaumés de la mer, malgré les vins de très bons crus, les cuisseaux de veau et les cuissots de chevreuil prodigués par l'amphitryon, fut un vrai guêpier," he began, declaiming three more paragraphs.

The guests handed in their papers, and Mérimée tallied the results. Over the course of 169 words, Napoleon III made 75 mistakes, Eugénie 62, and Alexandre Dumas, 24. The winner of the game was Prince Metternich of Austria, with 3 faults. Dumas, auto-chastising, turned to him and said, "When will you present yourself at the Academy, to teach us how to spell?"

MONDAYS, WEDNESDAYS, AND FRIDAYS, we have Luisa, a stout Venezuelan Frenchwoman with cantilevered gray curls. Luisa speaks quickly and correctly. She does not welcome questions. Every morning, she greets us—she's a *vous* woman—with what I come to think of as a Duchenne scowl.

Class opens briskly. We turn to chapter 2, "Come to My House!" The topic of discussion is cohabitation.

Luisa zeroes in on Satomi, the Japanese academic, who has yet to utter a word.

"Tell me about your living situation, Satomi."

"I live with my husband," Satomi says quietly. "He's American."

"Is he an ideal roommate?" Luisa asks.

"Yes, but sometimes he uses my toothbrush," Satomi says, daring to elaborate.

"That's an intimate violation!" Luisa barks.

Satomi withdraws like a slap bracelet.

Luisa turns to Scotty, the Alaskan.

"Scotty, what are the qualities of the ideal roommate?"

"They have to be nice," Scotty replies.

"And, for you, what is nice?"

"Friendly?"

"Friendly seems a little extreme," Luisa says, her eyebrow jerking up.

Scotty thinks for a moment.

"The ideal roommate shouldn't smoke?"

Most of the class nods in agreement. But there is sniggering from the corner, where the Italians sit en bloc.

"Yeah, maybe for you," one of them says. "You're not *our* ideal roommate."

Carlos, the Spanish bellboy, chimes in.

"Not someone bipolar."

"No!" comes the cry from the Italian corner. It's Cristina.

"I'm an artist," she says. "This concerns me. One day, I'm happy. One day, I'm not. I was living in Norway. I was a little depressed. I didn't want to talk to my roommates, and they were the type of person that if they asked, 'How was your day?' you had to say, 'I took the bus, I ate a sandwich.' After a week, we had to have a discussion about the fact that I wasn't very communicative. But their view of communication was exaggerated."

"Listen, it's a matter of respect," Carlos replies, fingering a black cord that he wears around his neck. "If you have a bad day, you don't have to put it on the other person."

Carlos is right, but he's driving me nuts with his inability to stop actually answering the questions, rather than merely demonstrating his ability to do so. When he's lost for words, he throws out filler—*tout ça, tout ça*—until he regains his bearings. He desperately wants us to know what he really thinks: that there is a lot of oriental influence in modern home decor, that bougainvillea is a beautiful flower, that the owners of pit bulls are not well educated. You say tomato, he says the problem these days is that when you ship food, it lacks vitamins. Tugging on his choker, he rambles on about the importance of positive thinking *et tout ça* until it's time for our coffee break.

I walk downstairs to get some air. Cristina is standing outside the building, dragging on a cigarette.

"I didn't know Norwegians were that cheerful," I say, trying to find some common ground.

"My roommates weren't Norwegian," she replies. "It was my half sister and my half sister's husband."

After the break, we resume the discussion. Lana raises her hand.

"My boyfriend—my ex—and I bought an apartment in Bosnia," she says. "But the problem was that we never fought. One day, a woman telephoned me and she said that she was with him. I told him about it, and he asked me how did I know it was true. I said that she had described our apartment—right down to the sheets on the bed."

Luisa, stone-faced, waits a minute before responding. "C'est la vie, non?"

. . .

DOMINIQUE SAYS that we can absorb French by osmosis. We should have the television or the radio on whenever we're home. I'm militant about following this piece of advice as—in inverse relationship to my daily needs—I can read and write and even speak in French much better than I can understand it when spoken. Bit by bit, the language is taking shape, definite articles and nouns and indirect objects and verbs and prepositional phrases hanging off subjects and predicates and predicate complements like a Calder mobile. Conjugations are coming along. To my delight, I can now distinguish among *un éléphant* (a male elephant), *une éléphant* (a female elephant), and *un éléphanteau* (a baby elephant of either gender).

English is a notoriously difficult language to pronounce. French—for me, at least—is an exceedingly tough language to hear. Every syllable is accented equally, making it difficult to figure out where words begin and end. I often tease Olivier about the way he says "can't remember"—"can tree member," as though he were describing a still life of soup, oak, and penis.

French words are connected by the liaison system, in which a word ending in a consonant links to the next one, if it begins in a vowel. The sentence "Je suis une étudiante qui n'a aucune difficulté de apprendre où on peut utiliser les liaisons," sounds, when spoken correctly, like "Juh sweezoonaytoodeeyante keena ohkoon deefeekultayduhprondruhoowon poo ootuhleezay lay leeayzon." In English, this is known as being drunk. French words are impressionable, a little bit fickle, behaving differently according to whom they're with. A French word, if all its friends did, would definitely jump off the Brooklyn Bridge.

Another fiction about learning a language is that you can become fluent by watching TV. But sitcoms and reality shows—with their fast, slangy dialogue and serial plots—are extremely hard to follow if you don't already know what's happening. I decide to start with the radio, which makes up for in elocution what it lacks in visual clues. Every morning I turn on Radio France Internationale. At first, I listen to the previous day's news in "français facile," following along with the transcript that RFI posts on the Internet every afternoon.

Français facile is, in fact, quite difficult. In *Eight Months on Ghazzah Street*, her novel about an Englishwoman who moves to Jeddah with her engineer husband, Hilary Mantel—an Englishwoman who moved to Jeddah with her engineer husband in 1983—describes the protagonist's efforts to learn Arabic. "Andrew took her to the bookshop at the Caravan Shopping Center," Mantel writes. "She bought a language tape, and a book to go with it, and during Jamadi al-awal she pored over this book, and set the careful slow voice of the language tutor echoing through [the apartment]. 'Good morning. Good morning, how are you? Well, praise be to God. Welcome! Will you drink coffee? How are your children? How is your wife?'" Despite her intelligence and industry—she's a cartographer by trade, with a surfeit of free time—she is strangely impotent. Arabic won't take.

Her frustration resonates with me. My efforts at French leave me feeling at once inert and exhausted, as though I've been dog-paddling in a pool of standing water. But as the weeks go by, the liaisons begin to sound less murky. I drop the script and start tuning in to the correct morning's broadcast, the *Sept neuf avec Patrick Cohen* on France Inter, a public radio station.

Trying to understand Patrick Cohen is an almost physical challenge—I have to concentrate my mental energy and then push with all my might, straining to make out the words the way one would to lift a dumbbell. Listening to one of Cohen's guests speak about the need for more women in positions of power at companies, I think how universal that conversation is. As I'm nodding along, the thought occurs perhaps that I've missed a feint or a negation that actually renders the entire argument the opposite of what I've understood it to be. What if I've got the right topic but the wrong stance, and the guest is actually *anti* female executives? An unreliable auditor, I can't trust what I'm hearing.

I let the conversation fade into gobbledygook, a break between sets. Afraid I'll atrophy if I rest too long, I insert my earphones and then turn on the hair dryer. I will learn French even if I too become half deaf.

A few weeks later I stumble into the bathroom, pulling the phone out of the pocket of my robe in my usual bleary routine. I put it on the counter, swipe to the RFI app, and press play. First four words: *nid d'oiseaux chanteurs.* No preamble. Patrick Cohen, I know immediately, is talking about a nest of songbirds.

That night Olivier's brother calls. Usually their conversations pass me by—I've missed years of ambient commentary, overheard plans—but this time little fragments of dialogue sing out, as though someone has fiddled with the volume knob on the background music to our life.

"Elle n'est pas très mobile, quoi," I hear Olivier say.

I don't know whom he's talking about, or why she's incapacitated. He seems to be saying "quoi" a lot. Even as it dawns on me that I may have pledged lifelong devotion to a man who ends every sentence with the equivalent of "dude," I'm taken by an eerie joy. Four years after having met Olivier, I'm hearing his voice for the first time.

WE'VE MADE IT THROUGH most of the winter without burning down the building. Downstairs, the iridologue is still shining a flashlight into people's eyeballs. We don't have much of a nightlife, but we do have s'mores, constructed with marshmallows I buy at the American store by which I am not employed. After I pass the Nest of Songbirds Test, Olivier and I get into the habit of spending Saturday nights in front of the fireplace, watching the French version of the singing competition *The Voice.*

In terms of format, *The Voice: la plus belle voix* is almost exactly the same as the American *Voice*, which itself is based on the Dutch *Voice*: blind auditions, battle rounds, violently swiveling chairs that look as though they're about to go flying out of their centripetal force. Instead of Adam Levine, Blake Shelton, Pharrell Williams, and Christina Aguilera, the judges are Florent Pagny, Garou, Mika, and Jenifer. Florent Pagny, the seventeenth-best-selling artist in France between 1955 and 2013, is a classically trained singer with a ponytail and a chest tattoo of a fleur-de-lis. The Québécois Garou made his name playing Quasimodo in the French musical *Notre-Dame de Paris.* Mika, an American-British-Lebanese-French pop star—partial to ascots and suspenders, waistcoats and epaulets—was nominated for a Best Dance Recording Grammy in 2008. Jenifer was on a reality show called *Star Academy* and seems, from the covers of the tabloids, to have been pregnant for two years.

The Voice: la plus belle voix is my favorite show because it's completely predictable. An aspiring star shows up, he talks to the camera about his dreams, he sings a song, his family cries, his dreams are either fulfilled or crushed. All I have to do is listen to a lot of Johnny Hallyday covers and decide whether the judges thought they were *pas mal* ("not bad," meaning "good") or *pas terrible* ("not bad," meaning "awful").

We get to know the judges. In the manner of the Mr. Men books, they each embody a single attribute. Garou is bland; Jenifer's nice; Mika's fun. We love Florent Pagny, who lives in Patagonia half of the year—Olivier because he once dated Vanessa Paradis, and I for his lunar air. Staring into the distance, stroking his goatee, he seems to be listening to the windpipes on some far-off steppe.

We're going for Manon Trinquier, a throaty Amy Winehouse lookalike from Narbonne. In the blind audition round, she does an awesomely maximal rendition of the Belgian star Stromae's hit "Formidable," turning the final verse into a blood-and-thunder spat-word aria.

"Si maman est chiante / C'est qu'elle a peur d'être mamie," I scream along, levitating from the couch as the song reaches its climax.

"Si papa trompe maman / C'est parce que maman vieillit, tiens," Olivier joins in.

I've never seen him like this. He's belting it out, Édith Piaf in a pullover.

"Pourquoi t'es tout rouge? Ben reviens, gamin!"

All of the judges except Mika swing around in their spaceship chairs. As Manon finishes in a lacy wail, Olivier and I high-five, collapsing breathless on the rug.

"Elle était formidable," Florent Pagny says.

Jenifer palms her face in excitement.

"Manon, tu es canon!"

Manon slays "Wrecking Ball" in the battle round, but she never quite recovers from a shaky "Ne Me Quitte Pas." It's becoming clear that "Kendji *le gitan*"—Kendji Girac, a seventeen-year-old of Roma ancestry—is the crowd favorite. He sings "Mad World," by Tears for Fears, with a backdrop of barrel fires.

"It's the first time he sings in English," the host says as the camera cuts to the judges, standing. "We have to be aware that it's extremely difficult to sing this song that you've chosen. But to be able to incarnate it with modesty, and at the same time conviction, it's difficult—and rare."

"And Kendji's done it," Mika says. "Frankly, he's done it."

Florent Pagny caresses his chin, smiling.

"Bravo l'artiste."

IT'S A FRIDAY. We're listening to a Mauritanian folk tale. There is a wise old man. He notices that his daughters have lately been wearing more revealing clothes. He summons them and seats them around him in a circle, then shows them his hands. The right one is open. In it, he holds an ounce of gold. The left one is closed.

"Choose one," he tells his daughters.

Without knowing what's in it, they all select the left fist.

"But you see that in my right hand there's an ounce of pure gold, while you don't know what's in the other one," the man says.

The daughters still want the one on the left.

Thus bidden, he opens it. There's nothing there except a lump of coal.

"You see, my children," he declares, "man always prefers that which hides itself from him."

Luisa presses stop on the tape deck and scans the classroom. "What do you think?" she says. "Lauren?"

"I think the Mauritanian folk tale is pretty sexist," I reply.

"Is that so? But why? There's a profound philosophical lesson here—that people should have a hidden side."

"Why doesn't he tell his sons that, then?"

"It's not sexist to say that a woman should have more mystery."

"I think that's sexist."

"It's not sexist," Cristina, the artist, says, cutting in. "It's about tradition versus modernity."

Luisa, warming to this interpretation, turns to Cristina and asks her to continue.

"Too open is not interesting," she says. "That's the moral of the story."

Carlos can't help himself.

"Man and woman are not the same!" he cries. "That's reality."

It's a pile-on. I know I should probably fold, but sixteen rounds of *The Voice* have emboldened me to brazen out the argument on my own.

"Reality can be sexist," I say, fixing Carlos with a stare. "What if this was Saudi Arabia instead of Mauritania?"

Carlos is, for a millisecond, speechless.

"Ladies," he says, regaining his composure. He opens his chest to the room, like a lawyer addressing a jury. "Do you prefer a man who shows it all, or who keeps a little hidden?"

"I think people should wear whatever they want," I say.

"No, but what if a guy is walking around in *collants*?"

Merde, what are *collants*? I whip out my little dictionary app like a gunslinger in a saloon fight.

"What do you think of a guy," Cristina is yelling, "who wears tights to show his intimate form?"

My pistol requires a password. I can't type fast enough. Lana raises a manicured hand.

"It's not the same for a man or a woman," she says.

Carlos replies, "That's why I asked what you ladies think."

"Women aren't the same as men," Lana continues. "They care what we wear. I care what he feels, what he thinks."

Luisa rustles her papers, trying to regain control of the conversation.

"Frank?" she says.

"Uhh."

After class, Cristina approaches me in the canteen.

"That was very American of you, what you said."

"Thanks," I say, sawing away at my veal cutlet.

Repeating "I think that's sexist" doesn't exactly qualify as rhetorical pyrotechnics. But I'm pleased that I've managed to say something that sounds reasonably like myself. Until now, I've thought of learning as something passive. I've been hoarding words as though they were rare doubloons, tucking them away in the velvet pouches of my cerebrum. But they're worthless, I realize, out of circulation. A language is the only subject you can't learn by yourself.

ONE SATURDAY, we drive up into the mountains. For the first time in my Alpine career, I'm not the worst skier in the party. The honor falls to our friend Ankit, who grew up in Sydney. It's his first time in the snow. He's arranged to spend a few hours with an instructor, to get the hang of the basics.

Olivier and Victoria, Ankit's girlfriend, are lifelong adepts of skiing and French, my tandem Genevan nemeses. I'm extremely jittery on the slopes, but after a winter in Switzerland, I can more or less keep up. We pass an easy morning surveying the runs—a roving isosceles triangle, me bringing up the vertex. From the lift, we catch a glimpse of Ankit sliding backward, electric yellow, down the bunny slope, as though he were streaking through an optical fiber.

We've made plans to meet for lunch at noon, at a restaurant the instructor has recommended. Olivier, Victoria, and I ski halfway down a bumpy red run and turn off toward a log cabin that's barely visible from the trail. Smoke is rising from the chimney. The path that leads to the cabin is steep and narrow. After veering several times into the drifts that line it, I give in to my survivalist instincts and snowplow the whole way down, kneecaps torqueing. We're waiting at the bottom when Ankit blazes into sight.

He's going fast and frantic. He takes a hard fall at the turnoff to the restaurant, but gamely dusts himself off. The path proves no easier for him to navigate than it was for me. But after a suite of brittle tumbles he arrives, standing, at the cabin's doorstep.

"Bravo, l'artiste!" I yell, letting out a cheer.

Olivier looks at me quizzically.

"Where did you get that?"

"La plus belle voix!"

Olivier is cracking up.

"You realize that's like going around saying, 'You're kind of pitchy, dog,' right?"

I hadn't realized. I'm just regurgitating what I've been fed. To be successful at learning a language, one has to undertake a form of time travel, regressing to a childlike state of unembarrassed receptivity, in order to stand a chance of turning into a respectable adult. The unformed speaker has no more way of evaluating her influences than a baby does her parents. She eats whatever they feed her whole. People are playing God, we say, when they arbitrate mortality, but what about vocabulary? The patrons of my French, I realize, have created me as fully as though out of bone and hair. There is so much power in giving words.

The gods can mess with you. An American friend, married to an Italian, tells me, "I remember that when I was learning, I was reading a lot of Svevo and speaking like a nineteenth-century Italian gentleman. My Roman friends delighted in my vocabulary. I kept saying 'wet nurse.' " In class, we complete a unit on law and order. I wonder if Migros has loosed a band of aspiring crime victims upon Geneva, reciting a series of identical complaints about swindles and scams, simply because we can. But play, and being played with, is part of the deal. With every screwup, every catchphrase I shout across a mountaintop, thinking it a commonplace, I feel my sense of who I am in French mature.

GOATS CAN DEVELOP regional accents. So can chaffinches and yellowhammers, whose dialect differences—city birds sing at a higher pitch, to reduce feedback from buildings—are more distinct than those of humans. French French, to the Swiss ear, sounds stiff, while Swiss French, to a French person, comes off as singsong. Much of the controversy seems to center around the words for 70, 80, and 90: *soixante-dix*, *quatre-vingts*, and *quatre-vingt-dix* in French French, simplified by the Swiss—perhaps as a courtesy to their bankers—to *septante*, *huitante*, and *nonante*.

"*Quatre-vingt-dix* is not useful," Dominique decrees.

"*Nonante* is not elegant," Luisa says, the next day. (On this she is in accord with the Zairean dictator Mobutu Sese Seko, who fired any civil servant who dared to utter it.)

Soon it's time for our oral presentations. The majority of my classmates choose to speak about their hometowns. As March melts into April, we are transported to Berlin, Buenos Aires, Verona, Lake Como. It's hard for me to believe that I've ended up in the same place as the sons and daughters of the cities of which I once collected postcards, which so enticed and frightened me, as my classmates played *futbol* in their alleys or ate schnitzel in their rathskellers. Even Lana's Banja Luka, with its fort and its discotheques, possesses a certain grandeur. When my turn comes, I decide to forgo Wilmington and talk about living in French.

"Today, I'm going to speak about the differences, or the lack thereof, among the world's languages," I say. "There are two schools of thought on the subject, one that suggests that each language expresses itself uniquely, and the other that holds that all the languages are variations on a universal theme."

I grab a piece of chalk and write on the blackboard:

> I speak Spanish to God, Italian to women, French to men, and German to my horse.
>
> —Charles V

"Sorry, Frank," I say.

Dominique likes my presentation, even if she finds it a little abstruse.

"I think you are in a period where you want to make some more complex phrases," she says.

"I got a *nonante-cinq* on my *exposé*," I brag that night in the kitchen.

"Argh!" Olivier says, recoiling. "You cannot say 'nonante'!"

"Ta mère en string panthère," I fire back, entering the adolescent phase of my life in French.

OLIVIER AND I are sitting in the back of a twelve-passenger van in Tromsø, Norway. We've gone there, 217 miles north of the Arctic Circle, to try to see the northern lights. We only have three nights, so we've signed up with Marianne's Heaven on Earth Aurora Chaser Tours, Tromsø's hardest-core aurora-hunting outfit. Unlike the big bus tours that ferry tourists to preassigned viewing points night after night, MHOEACT prides itself on being a nimble operation, able to follow the skies on the fly. For 1,350 NOK—around $200—we've been promised snowsuits, reflector vests, headlamps, heat pads for feet and hands, gloves, hats, socks, boots, professional twelve-spike ice crampons, and "hot and cold food most nights sometimes heated over an open fire." We've brought our passports, as instructed. "We have no limits to where we might travel to find the aurora," the brochure reads; "200 km radius, Island hopping or North, South, East or West to Finland or Sweden."

It's five o'clock, two hours and forty-five minutes after sunset. The temperature is minus three. We're sitting in a van outside the Tromsø post office, waiting for the rest of the group to show up. I'm not surprised they're late. There is absolutely nothing to do in Tromsø, which makes it a lot of fun. Earlier in the day, Olivier and I marveled at the icebreakers in the harbor and took the briefest of peeks at Tromsø's wooden cathedral before running down the street—our jeans turning hard as plaster in the cold—to a bar serving wine and soup. There, the bartender told us about Norwegian speeding tickets, which carry a fine of 10 percent of one's annual income. We flipped through the Routard guide—the francophone Fodor's—which seemed at least as concerned about the food situation in Norway as with the northern lights. Routard warned that Norway is the capital of *malbouffe*—"bad food," such as hamburgers, hot dogs, kebabs, pizzas, and meatballs—"all with an air *un peu road movie made in USA*."

"The *pain aux raisins*, with glazed sugar and a touch of cream or sweet butter, are not bad, but, on the other hand, the brioches are insipid," I read aloud.

The guide seemed to think that the Norwegians may have even been responsible for the *malbouffe* in the United States.

"Eternal question of the chicken or the egg," I continued. "Let us not forget that the US is composed of the immigrants of many nations, a fair amount of whom come from Northern Europe."

Eventually the stragglers arrive and climb into the van. Marianne, a sturdy, affectless woman in fatigues and a patched sweater, is sitting in the passenger seat, looking at weather maps. Occupying the driver's seat is her boyfriend, George, a distracted Scot who blew into Tromsø a few years earlier on a camping trip.

George hits the gas and speeds out of the parking lot. For hours we circle around Norway's icy highways as Marianne growls into a walkie-talkie, communicating with a network of scouts. Sometime after 8:00, George careens into a rest area. We park, and the gear is distributed. Swaddled like mummies, we tumble out of the van.

The group disperses across a dark field. Olivier and I are standing side by side. Every once in a while we bump up against each other, as imperceptibly as bubble-wrapped glasses in a box. We look up. It's the aurora borealis: a chemical green smear, like a glow stick leaking across the dark.

We admire the lights at length while the photographers in the group make long-exposure shots, leaving their shutters open for fifteen minutes at a time. At 9:00, they are still beautiful but faint and, in a way, underwhelming. The aurora borealis, it turns out, is perhaps alone among natural phenomena in being more vivid in pictures than to the naked eye. By 11:00 the temperature has reached minus nine. We don't know where we are, or when we're going back. Marianne and George are rapt in their own camera gear. Eventually I retreat to the van, where Olivier unzips his polar suit and cradles my frozen feet to his chest like wounded birds.

Midnight goes by. George remembers he's supposed to light a fire. We get out and sit in the snow, drinking frigid cocoa, as he attempts to thaw a pack of Vienna sausages on a wobbly rack. Finally we return to the van, along with a Chinese woman and a pair of shivering Australians. We sit there, huddled, making intermittent conversation. We're starting to wonder if there's a safe word.

Marianne, having at last noticed our collectively waning attention, approaches and opens the door, her headlamp shining like an accusation.

"You're not watching the northern lights," she says.

"We're not," we answer.

"Why?" she asks, sounding hurt.

"Elle est folle, non?" I say to Olivier as Marianne wanders away, neck cocked toward the sky.

Olivier agrees with my diagnosis.

"Ouais, elle est complétement maboule."

I put my head on his shoulder. He finds a plastic tarpaulin and pulls it around our knees like a quilt.

It is perhaps not what the literary critic Marc Fumaroli had in mind when he wrote of "the banquet of the minds of which France was long the expert hostess, and whose memory will never be effaced," extolling French as "the modern language of the mind's clandestinity." But nonetheless I feel a sly sense of enfranchisement, a growing ownership of a quality that has long estranged me even as I've yearned to possess it. *La complicité*—you hear it all the time in French. *La complicité entre eux*, *une relation très complice*. It had always struck me as a weirdly dark encomium. I was put off by its air of codependency, even while being intrigued by the naughtiness it implied. Suddenly I get it: we're bank robbers, perpetrators of an improbable heist. A long relationship between the right people is a sort of brilliant crime.

"Elle est dingue," I say, exhausting my mental thesaurus of words for "crazy," wanting to make the moment last.

We are beginning to be a French couple, trading undetected confidences in the back of a twelve-passenger van. Tomorrow we will wake up and sneer at Tromsø's insipid brioches!

A MEMORY CAN BE A long-exposure photograph, the scene it captures becoming clear only over the course of years. An image comes to me: a restaurant in London, steak, a long table, some kind of bordello theme. Olivier and me, very early days. We're there with some of his crowd, everyone French. At the end of the night, we're all saying good-bye. The friend I've heard Olivier speak about the most says something funny. "I love you!" I gush.

We get in a taxi. Olivier is apoplectic. I chalk this up to a jealousy problem, tallying a mark in my mental column of cons. But his anger stings, especially in that my effusiveness has been a conscious effort to demonstrate an investment in his world, to show warmth to the people who mean something to him. I insist that "I love you!" isn't a come-on but a nicety, an unmissably hyperbolic "You're hilarious," or "That's great." I don't know then that *aimer*, "to love," is in French the realm of deep feeling. (There's a separate form, *aimer bien*, for "to like.") "The girls nowadays indulge in such exaggerated statements that one never can tell what they *do* mean," L. M. Montgomery writes in *Anne of the Island*. "It wasn't so in my young days. *Then* a girl did not say she *loved* turnips, in just the same tone as she might have said she loved her mother or her Saviour." I don't know that you still can't do that in French.

I don't know, either, that it's not just Olivier and me stuck in some sort of verbal deadlock, that English and French are opposing systems as much as they are languages—the former global, convenient, and casual; the latter particular, hierarchical, and painstaking. I have no way of foreseeing that French will reshape the contours of my relationships, that I won't always consider people intimates until proven not to be. I love my parents, my friends, my colleagues, the woman who gives me extra guacamole at Chipotle, hydrangeas, podcasts, clean sheets. Olivier has only ever loved me.

Another restaurant: Geneva, years later, watery mojitos, a wagyu beef burger in a tall glass cloche. We're there with a group organized by Olivier's boss. I'm sitting next to him. He's English. We talk about cricket, a sport of which I'm totally ignorant. Eventually something comes up that requires the input of Olivier, who's sitting at the other end of the table.

"Bébé" isn't going to cut it. But neither is a massacre. I'm facing the same problem one faces when ordering a gyro sandwich: say his name correctly and sound like an asshole; say it how everyone else does and betray my hard-won knowledge, sacrificing integrity to a false tact. I feel as though I'm being asked to declare an allegiance, to plant a flag on the terrain of myself, merely by opening my mouth.

"Oh-lee-vyay?" I say, cupping my lips tight and gentle around the syllables, as though they're eggs that might crack.

Five

THE CONDITIONAL
Le Conditionnel

HAD FRANCO NOT COME to power in 1939, Olivier might have spoken Spanish. His maternal grandmother came from a bourgeois family in Barcelona. (They spoke Catalan.) His Aragonian maternal grandfather—a schoolteacher, though his parents had wanted him to be a priest—was an atheist anarchist. When the civil war broke out, he joined the Republican Army as an officer. After the Republicans' defeat, he sought refuge in France, where he worked in the resistance movement. In the fall of 1944 he was part of a band of six thousand *guérilleros* who invaded Spain at the Aran Valley, intending to reconquer the territory. After their defeat, he led twenty-two survivors on a month-long retreat through the Pyrenees, crossing Andorra to arrive at Foix. Later he became a local councilman, and an Esperanto enthusiast. He died before I met Olivier, but I wondered whether his experiences in the war had left him with a desire to try to piece back together the map that nationalism had dissected, to reunite Europe through a common tongue.

One summer night, sitting in her garden, I asked Violeta about him.

"He was an anarchist," she began.

Before she could finish reciting his biography, Teddy chimed in.

"Mi parolas Esperanton!"

"Pardon?" I said.

"I speak Esperanto too," he continued, in French. "They had a class at the naturist resort my first wife and I used to go to in the sixties."

"It was an ideology," Violeta said.

"A way to reconnect mankind," Teddy added.

"The Esperanto or the nudism?"

Teddy said that he'd reluctantly abandoned Esperanto—nobody spoke it—but his interest in naturism was still going strong. He and Violeta, in fact, owned a vacation condo in Cap d'Agde, a clothes-optional resort on the Mediterranean. Before going to bed, I typed "Cap d'Agde" into Google. "A family destination that offers many equipments and activities to children and parents," the town's official website read. The unofficial website had a somewhat different take: "Originally Cap d'Agde was the domain of nudists and naturists, but swingers seem to have taken over the place bit by bit." At once I understood why all the world finds Americans puritanical. I was wondering how you say in Esperanto, "Ben Stiller, get a load of this."

The curse of Babel continued to bedevil our household. A friend of Olivier's, a *parisienne* who worked in fashion PR, was coming to visit us in Geneva. I spent days planning the menu, requisitioning the best lamb, stuffing the lamb with saffron rice, stressing out over which pâtisserie I'd go to for tiny *tartes* and *fondants*. (The how-to-be-a-French-person guides I'd read the year before assured me that store-bought desserts were totally acceptable.)

The dinner came off well. The meat was tender. I served the salad as a palate cleanser, in the French way, and after that, a selection of cheeses of different textures, levels of pungency, and varieties of milk. The desserts were a hit. Once we'd lingered a while at the table, we moved to the living room, where we lit a fire and watched as the flames pulled like taffy toward the flue.

For my benefit, we spoke in English. Christine, Olivier's friend, was complaining about some British colleagues.

"'Hey, lads,' it makes me insane," Olivier joined in.

I listened as it became clear that my dinner partners believed that a group they called "Anglo-Saxons"—comprising a culture that united Britain, its commonwealths, and former colonies—were engaged in some sort of global conspiracy.

France, Britain, and America: what a love triangle. I was reminded of a letter I'd seen in a museum exhibit, an internal memo that went around the British Foreign Office in 1941. "We are regarded as a cold-blooded, calculating people, and our failure to show warmth—to 'say it with flowers'—is perhaps the main reason why American respect for us never quite ripens into a warm, uncalculating friendship—such as they have felt for the French," it read. "If we could, for once in our lives, shed our caution and offer our most precious possession to our best friends, then the effect would be incalculable, both to-day and in the future." The writer wanted to make a permanent gift to the American people of the Lincoln Cathedral's Magna Carta, which had been a sensation at the New York World's Fair. Being an American, I had found the "for once in our lives" so poignant, suggestive in its mustachioed primness of a bureaucrat who, sensing the end of days, has finally worked up the nerve to cut in on a dance. I read on. Being an American, I had been had. The bureaucrat, in the last line of the letter, said it with mordant superiority: "And, after all, we possess four copies of Magna Carta."

"Just look at the list of countries the NSA spies on," Olivier was saying. "It's only Anglo-Saxons that the US trusts."

"How exactly does India fit into this scheme?" I asked.

He and Christine looked at each other as though the answer were too obvious to be worth articulating.

"South Africa?" I continued.

"Americans don't like to be reminded that they were part of an empire, do they?" one of them said.

Having had enough, I got up, slammed the door, not very chicly, and went to bed.

SCHNAPSIDEE—the way a German would describe a plan he'd hatched under the influence of alcohol. *Pilkunnussija*—Finnish for "comma fucker," a grammar pedant. In Mundari, *ribuy-tibuy* refers to the sight, sound, and motion of a fat person's buttocks. *Jayus*, in Indonesian, denotes a joke told so poorly that people can't help but laugh. *Knullrufs* is Swedish for postsex hair. *Gumusservi* means moonlight shining on the water in Turkish. *Culaccino* is the Italian word for the mark left on a table by a cold glass.

Words like these are marvelous. We make lists of them, compile them into treasuries, trade them over any dinner table at which holders of more than one passport have convened. (The German, armed with *Kummerspeck*—"grief bacon"—will always win the day.) They're fun to say. They're funny to think about, in their Seinfeldian particularity. They expand

and concentrate the world, making it bigger-spirited while at the same time more specific.

We like to think that the lexicon of a language reveals broad truths about its speakers. The wine will flow, and the Japanese guest will mention *komorebi*, the sunlight filtering through the leaves of trees, and the Frenchman will offer *l'appel du vide*, the urge to jump off the side of a cliff, and there will be collective acknowledgment of the aesthetic qualities of the Japanese, and the nihilistic ones of the French. But the idea that untranslatable words prove that speakers of different languages experience the world in radically different ways is as dubious as it is popular, originating from "the great Eskimo vocabulary hoax"—the notion that Eskimo has fifty or eighty or a hundred words for snow.

Eskimo is not a language but a group of them, comprising the Inuit and Yupik families, spoken from Greenland to Siberia. Nor, as the linguist Geoffrey Pullum explains, are they actually especially rich in snow terminology. What they are rich in is suffixes, which allow their speakers to build endless variations upon a small base of root words. (If you're tallying derivations, Eskimos also have a multitude of words for "sun.") Sticking strictly to lexemes, or minimal meaningful units of language, Anthony C. Woodbury has cataloged about fifteen distinct snow words in one Eskimo language, Central Alaskan Yupik—roughly the same number as there are in English. A cartoon, mocking our credulity, features two Eskimos. One asks the other, "Did you know that in Hampstead"—a neighborhood in North London—"they have twenty words for bread?"

Even if Eskimos did possess a voluminous vocabulary for snow, or Hampsteaders for bread, it wouldn't prove that they were subject to some separate reality, that their language sliced up the world into mutually unavailable porterhouses and *araignées.* Lepidopterists have names for the behavior that butterflies exhibit at damp spots (puddling) and for the opening of the silk gland found on the caterpillar's lower lip (spinneret). Architects can distinguish between arrowslits, bartizans, and spandrels, while pilots speak of upwash and adverse yaw. New words are created every day by people who are able to comprehend their meanings before they exist. Novel language can be a function of time as well as space. Czech speakers came up with *prozvonit*—the act of calling a cell phone and hanging up after one ring so that the other person will call you back, saving you money—because cell phones were invented, not because they were Czech. Even if languages express certain concepts more artfully, or more succinctly, it's precisely because we recognize the phenomena to which they refer that we're delighted by *knullrufs* and *Kummerspeck.*

A language carries within it a culture, or cultures: ways of thinking and being. With the exception of Olivier, I spoke American English with the people to whom I was closest, who spoke American English back to me. For most of my life, I had assumed that Americanness agreed with me, because I had never questioned it. My alienations were localized, smallerbore. In North Carolina, I craved the immensity of New York. In New York, I longed for the intimacy of North Carolina. It wasn't that I didn't like either culture. I loved them both. But my family's trajectory over the course of three generations—north, south, and north again, a chevron of opportunity and discontent—had left me feeling that I could claim neither place as fully my own. In one, I was an arriviste; in the other, some part of me would always be a bumpkin, marveling at the existence of "doorman buildings" and thinking the phrase "plus one" a little mean. In ways, I felt that I had already learned a new language, "picked it up," like Zadie Smith, "in college, along with the unabridged *Clarissa* and a taste for port."

"Why do people want to adopt another culture?" Alice Kaplan, the French scholar, writes. "Because there's something in their own they don't like, that doesn't *name them*." For me, French wasn't an uncomplicated refuge. I was coming at the language, I think, from the opposite angle to Kaplan: I had accidentally become the proprietor of a life suffused by French, and for all its charms, there was something I didn't like in *it*.

In French the grid was divided differently, between public and private, rather than polite and rude. At first I felt its emphasis on discrimination, its relentless taxonomizing, as an almost ethical defect. French—the language and the culture—was so doctrinaire, so hung up on questions of form. The necessity of classifying each person one came across as *vous* or *tu*, outsider or insider, potential foe or friend, seemed at best a pomposity and at worst an act of paranoia. The easy egalitarianism of English tingled like a phantom limb. French could feel as "old and cold and settled in its ways" a place to live as Joni Mitchell's Paris. One day I bought a package of twenty *assiettes pour grillades* and ached for America, where you could use your large white paper plates for whatever the hell you wanted.

Like Mark Twain—who translated one of his stories from French back into English, to produce the thrice-baked "The Frog Jumping of the County of Calaveras"—I found the language comically unwieldy. In its reluctance to disobey itself, it often seemed effete. One French newspaper had a column that recapitulated the best tweets of the week in more characters than they took to write. The biggest ridiculousism I ever came across was "dinde gigogne composée d'une dinde partiellement désossée, farcie d'un canard partiellement désossé, lui-même farci d'un poulet partiellement désossé"—that is to say, turducken.

Even if *muruaneq*—Yupik word for soft, deep fallen snow—was basically powder, the question tantalized me: Does each language have its own worldview? Do people have different personalities in different languages? Every exchange student and maker of New Year's resolutions hopes that the answer is yes. More than any juice cleanse or lottery win or career switch, a foreign language adumbrates a vision of a parallel life. The fantasy is that learning one activates a latent alter ego, righting a linguistic version of having been switched at birth. Could I, would I, become someone else if I spoke French?

THE ACADEMY IS VICIOUSLY SPLIT on the question of whether one's language shapes one's worldview. The debate examines language at the structural level, seeking to determine whether the distinctions that each one obliges its speakers to make—what they *must* say, rather than what they *may* say—result in differences in memory, perception, and practical skills. So far, no one can definitively say whether Montaigne's parents were onto something in insisting that he be brought up in Latin, so that he could learn to think like the ancients. Depending on whom you ask, languages are either prescription glasses (changing the way you see the world) or vanity contact lenses (basically negligible). As one of the major unsolved mysteries of human cognition, the subject inspires theories as impassioned as they are irreconcilable.

Linguistic relativism—the idea that languages possess and inculcate different ways of thinking—gained purchase in the eighteenth century, spreading from the Romantics in France to their counterparts in Germany. As critics of the Enlightenment, the Romantics expressed a preference for the emotional, local, and subjective by adopting the creed of nationalism, which held that the state's legitimacy rested in the unity of the people it governed. Nationalism, in their reckoning, was a means of spiritual renewal. Language was the font of national identity. "One of the most interesting inquiries into the history and manifold characteristics of the human understanding and heart would be found in a philosophical comparison of languages; since on each of these the mind and character of a people are strongly impressed," Johann Gottfried Herder wrote, adding, "The genius of a people is nowhere more decisively indicated than in the physiognomy of its speech." Like phrenologists measuring skulls, the Romantics sought to extrapolate the characters of peoples from their linguistic contours.

At Columbia in the early twentieth century, the anthropologist Franz Boas revived the Romantic interest in the diversity of languages, laying the foundations for linguistic relativism's modern form. (It was Boas, in fact, who first mentioned Eskimos and snow.) His protégé Edward Sapir went on to become a seminal figure in the foundation of the field of linguistics, producing studies of such languages as Nootka, Sarcee, and Chinook. "The fact of the matter is that the 'real world' is to a large extent unconsciously built up on the language habits of the group," he wrote. "No two languages are ever sufficiently similar to be considered as representing the same social reality."

Sapir trained Benjamin Lee Whorf, as strange and poignant a figure as American intellectual life has ever produced. Whorf was born in 1897 in Winthrop, Massachusetts. After an undistinguished undergraduate career in the chemical engineering department at MIT, he became a fire prevention inspector with the Hartford Fire Insurance Company, specializing in the underwriting of buildings with automatic sprinklers. Whorf was a Methodist, of English stock. During a crisis of faith, he became interested in Jewish mysticism, particularly as manifested by the Hebrew alphabet, which occultists had for centuries picked apart and spun around and recombined, believing it to hold the secret to man's original tongue. In 1926 Whorf added Aztec to his self-imposed, self-taught curriculum. In 1928 he took up Mayan. His quest to unearth the lost meanings of letters, to rediscover a linguistic city of gold, obsessed him to the point that his friends complained that he passed them by in the street, offering no sign of recognition. Appearing at the Twenty-Third International Congress of Americanists, seemingly out of nowhere, he dazzled the establishment with a translation of an Aztec manuscript long held to be impenetrable. On its strength, he received a grant to pursue his research in Mexico. The fire insurance company, the *Hartford Courant* noted, agreed to grant him a leave of absence.

Passing his days at smelting plants and tanneries, Whorf worked his way into New England's elite intellectual circles, enrolling in Sapir's graduate seminar in American Indian linguistics at Yale. (His younger brother, Richard, moved to California and eventually directed *The Beverly Hillbillies.*) In 1940 he announced an attention-getting discovery: the Hopi language, he said, had no linear sense of time. He based this claim on several peculiarities of Hopi grammar, including the fact that its verbs did not indicate past, present, and future tense, per se. Rather, they marked validity, so that "He ran" would be rendered in Hopi as either "Wari" (running, a statement of fact) or "Era wari" (running, a statement of fact from memory). Presenting his findings as "the linguistic relativity principle," Whorf heralded a "new physics," in which speakers of different languages were compelled by their grammars to different experiences of externally identical phenomena. "We dissect nature along lines laid down by our native languages," he wrote.

Whorf died of cancer the next year, at the age of forty-four. In the decades to follow, some of his ideas were proven to be incorrect or overstated—among them the Hopi concept of time—but even the most prescient were vulnerable to distortion. In the 1950s the "Sapir-Whorf hypothesis," stripped of its original subtleties, became shorthand for a sort of brute conflation of speech and thought. A shelter under which various canards about language congregated, it was marked for demolition by the 1960s, when Noam Chomsky and his theory of universal grammar came along.

Language, according to Chomsky, is a biological instinct. We are each equipped with a grammatical toolkit; all we have to do to start building is to be born a human being. In Chomsky's view, speech is as independent of culture as breathing or walking. The differences among languages are so trivial that each one of the seven thousand tongues spoken on earth would register as a mere dialect to a visitor from Mars. Rendered in a mathematical logic that cared little for igloos or clocks, Chomsky's ideas were revolutionary, and then they were consensual. By 1994, when the Harvard psychologist and linguist Steven Pinker published *The Language Instinct*, an "obituary" for the Sapir-Whorf hypothesis, the concept of linguistic relativity had taken on an air of disrepute and even infamy.

People know how to speak like spiders know how to spin webs, Pinker argued, drawing much of his evidence from studies of the extraordinary abilities of children to acquire language without formal instruction. "The idea that thought is the same thing as language," he asserted, "is an example of what can be called a conventional absurdity: a statement that goes against all common sense but that everyone believes because they dimly recall having heard it somewhere and because it is so pregnant with implications." The Sapir-Whorf hypothesis, even if he had rather distorted it, was to Pinker a crock, a folk belief of the same dim hordes who took it as fact that lemmings commit mass suicide and the *Boy Scout Manual* is the world's best-selling book. Benjamin Lee Whorf, one scholar wrote, had undergone a demotion from unlikely hero to one of "the prime whipping boys of introductory texts on linguistics."

THE ACADÉMIE FRANÇAISE *s'en branle* about Noam Chomsky. (In French you don't say "could give a rat's ass," you say "jerk yourself off.") Founded in 1635 by Cardinal Richelieu to "clean the language of all the filth it has contracted," the academy is the high authority on questions of what is or is not French. Richelieu modeled the institution on private clubs of language lovers that gathered at the Hôtel de Rambouillet. Today, its forty members are novelists, poets, philosophers, journalists, historians, doctors, attorneys, biologists, clergymen, and politicians. They are elected for life. In order to gain admittance, they must apply to fill a specific seat, whose previous holder they eulogize in a public speech.

Voltaire, Victor Hugo, and Louis Pasteur were academicians, as have been five heads of state, including Valéry Giscard d'Estaing, the president of the French Republic from 1974 to 1981, who currently occupies seat 16. Baudelaire, however, was excluded on moral grounds; Moliere was snubbed for being an actor; Zola applied twenty-four times and was rejected on each.

"Willy-nilly, in the twenty-first century as in the eighteenth, anyone who wants to shake off the leaden cloak of conformism and mass communication, anyone who discovers that he wants before dying to participate in a civilized conversation, the image on this earth of *nostra conversatio quae est in coelis*, does so in French," the academician Marc Fumaroli has written (at least according to his translator, whose decision to use "willy-nilly" rather than "whether one likes it or not" provokes curiosity). The academy's motto: *à l'immortalité*. The notion that language is universal is about as plausible in its cosmology as a Champagne from Belize.

Technically, the academy's job is to produce a dictionary. Historically, it has not shone at this task, publishing nine editions over the course of four centuries. Its true role is custodial rather than creative. It acts as an overprotective guardian to the French language, fretting over who she's gone out with, when she's coming home, how she'll navigate a crude world without compromising her dignity. The academy can be reactionary: in 1997 it rejected the adoption of feminine versions of professional titles, arguing that *la ministre* and *la juge* belonged properly not to female ministers and judges but to the wives of their male colleagues. Even though the grammatical principles behind the position were sound—all French nouns are either masculine or feminine, denotations that have nothing to do with their referents' genitalia—the academy's stand confirmed its reputation as a bastion of crusty hauteur. The goal, it was clear, was to preserve the purity of the language—less a French well punished than one hardly touched.

The chief debaucher of French, of course is English, a loud-mouthed vulgarian who made his fortune selling cola and computers. French and English have coexisted and crossbred for as long as they've been spoken. But after World War II—as French lost its sinecure as the language of diplomacy and was forced to concede to English in the realms of film and aviation—English morphed from acquaintance to antagonist. "As befits a hard-working people, the French have no word for 'week end,'" the *International Herald Tribune* reported in 1959. (An editorial writer, perpetuating the they-don't-have-a-word-for fallacy today, could just as easily claim that the French are so lazy that, to them, there's no difference between a weekend and a workday.) The paper continued, "So they have taken it over bodily from English, pronouncing it in English and enjoying it just as much as anyone else. Similar examples come to mind readily—'bifteck' for beefsteak, for instance, and 'gongstair' for gangster. But the English flavoring of French has begun to get out of hand, apparently, and in some Parisian circles is even becoming quite chic, or, as we say here, chick."

Five years later the critic René Étiemble published *Parlez-vous franglais?*, a polemic against the English language and Anglo-Saxon culture, "that air-conditioned nightmare." It aimed to combat the vogue for English through ridicule: the entire first chapter was written in a hideous pastiche of "*cette variété* new look *du babélien*." The book helped to galvanize the feeling that language was a zero-sum game, that gains by English were a loss for French. Even as linguists thrilled to the ingenuity with which French speakers assimilated English—and, in the postcolonial era, languages such as Arabic and Wolof—and made it their own, eminences fretted that the dilution of the language would lead irretrievably to the deterioration of the culture, to which it was so dearly linked.

The central control of a pure French by Parisian authorities is a myth: Kinshasa is the world's second-largest French-speaking city. But it is a powerful one in France, with its tendency to privilege consistency over innovation. At the time of the French Revolution, only half of France's population spoke French fluently. Of the other half, 25 percent—speakers of regional languages such as Provençal and Breton—had no French whatsoever. (Even by the beginning of World War II, one out of two French people still claimed a regional language as their mother tongue.) In the nineteenth century, the government established universal education. It went on a standardization spree, purging the language of variations in grammar and spelling. Publishers joined in, issuing scrubbed versions of the French classics. "This linguistic revisionism fed (and still feeds) a quasi-religious belief among francophones that the French language had been *fixé* (set) since the time of Louis XIV," Julie Barlow and Jean-Benoît Nadeau write. Charles de Gaulle was drawing on this heritage when, in 1966, citing "the bastardization of French vocabulary," he created the Haut Comité Pour la Défense et l'Expansion de la Langue Française. The Bas-Lauriol law of 1975 restricted the use of foreign words in business and advertising. By the time a more muscular version of it was enacted in 1994, famously dictating that 40 percent of the music played on the radio be sung in French, the battle against English represented a major front in France's culture wars, reliably bolstering political careers and launching best sellers.

Something about French is embarrassing to English speakers. Its sounds are too sensually mouth-contorting, its constructions too pompously fervid, with all those loopy clauses and long words. If we approach the language with a sense of abashment—P. G. Wodehouse immortalized "the shifty hang-dog look of an Englishman about to speak French"—French speakers treat English with the sort of high-flown outrage that we most love to mock. The protests are both so indignant and so quixotic. It's hard to suppress a smirk upon reading the demand of a group of striking Air France pilots: "Stopper toute propagation abusive de l'anglais." (*Stopper* not exactly being a canonical French verb.) Then there are the petitioning employees of the Carrefour supermarket of Nîmes-Sud, fuming, "Why this orgy of English words? Would we be under an Anglo-American protectorate?" all because they have to sell products called Bootstore, Top Bike, and Tex Fashion Express. Does anyone really think that French teenagers, per the academy's diktat, are going to trade out *sexting* for sending *textos pornographiques*?

It's easy to caricature the French as language hypochondriacs, but they are closer to hemophiliacs—a population that is especially sensitive to a genuine threat. French sees itself as not only an alternative to English but the most viable conduit of a competing value system. Calling on his compatriots in 2013 to boycott businesses that advertised in English, the philosopher Michel Serres argued that the increasing ubiquity of English was a cause of inequality: "Now the dominant class speaks English and French has become the language of the poor."

The complaint is not just a French one. "English is not a language. It is a class," Aatish Taseer recalls a Hindi-speaking friend—an aspiring Bollywood actor, refused work for his lack of English—telling him, in an essay called "How English Ruined Indian Literature." The argument is powerful. It applies easily to the rest of the world, with globalization creating a caste of linguistic have-nots. Boutros Boutros-Ghali, the former United Nations secretary general, has said that "much in the way democracy within a state is based on pluralism, democracy between states must be based on pluralingualism." Linguistic diversity, then, is a check on political monoculture. It is as unhealthy for the global community to rely too heavily on one language as it is to mass-cultivate a single crop.

In *The Search for a Perfect Language*, Umberto Eco makes a moving account of man's efforts, over the course of two millennia, to "heal the wound of Babel." They have been legion, running from the brilliant to the crackpot: Dante's illustrious vernacular, the *ars magna* of the Majorcan martyr Raymond Llull, the steganographers' codes, the Rosicrucians' "magick writing," Volapük, Interlingua. The quest to rediscover or to create a universal language has most often been a utopian project, but it is not without darker possibilities. In 1966 Leslie Stevens shot *Incubus*, a black-and-white Esperanto horror movie. Starring William Shatner—he would soon confront the Klingon language as Captain Kirk—as a soldier seduced by a succubus, the film premiered at the San Francisco Film Festival, where a group of Esperanto speakers showed up at the screening. "Anytime they thought things were not pronounced correctly," one of the producers recalled, "they screamed and laughed and carried on like *maniacs* and no one else could understand *why*." As Orwell knew, cooperation is not possible without communication, but neither is totalitarianism. One wonders what form global terrorism would take without global English as its vector.

In 1984—this really was the year—the Office of Nuclear Waste Isolation hired the linguist Thomas A. Sebeok to try to solve the problem of "nuclear semiotics": how to warn the humans ten thousand years in the future that they would be treading on radioactive wastelands. Sebeok produced a report titled *Communication Measures to Bridge Ten Millennia.* In it, he rejected electrical signals (they needed an uninterrupted power supply), olfactory messages (they wouldn't last long enough), pictograms (they would be as ambiguous as cave paintings are to us), and simply rendering the message in every known language and sign system (even if one of them managed to survive, it would have decayed beyond comprehensibility). The best hope, he concluded, would be to initiate an "atomic priesthood" of storytellers, charged with perpetuating over three hundred generations a folklore of danger that would last as long as uranium.

To GET TO THE WORD FACTORY, you cross the Seine at the Pont du Carrousel, wade through the Jardin des Tuileries—gravel gone porridgy in the late-fall dank—and take a right at the Louvre onto rue Saint-Honoré. Number 182 is the Ministry of Culture and Communication, situated in a former warehouse clad in a silvery mesh that recalls a cross between chain mail and fishnet stockings. On a November morning, blown-up photographs of the soldiers of 1914 filled the ground-floor windows, advertising the launch of an online archive that would allow citizens to search for their forebears among the dead of France. Public bikes serried near the entrance. Passing under a tumid *tricolore*, I went in and approached the information desk, explaining to the officer behind it that I was there for a 9:45 meeting. When he asked for a piece of identification, I produced a card that read "Füherausweis—Permis de conduire—Licenza di condurre—Permiss da manischar—Driving Licence." It featured my face, overlaid by holographic Swiss crosses. My last name was Irish. My middle name was German. I was speaking French, a language in which people often thought Lauren—easily confusable with Laurent—referred to a man.

It was always a strange thing, handing over my Swiss permit. All it technically said was that I was authorized to drive a motor vehicle in any of Switzerland's twenty-six cantons, with or without a trailer, but it seemed to mean much more. I wondered why passports and drivers' licenses are objects of such fascination; why we are apt to pass them around, giggling at one another's expressions, scrutinizing birthdates, rapt at such banalities as eye color and height; why a friend's headshot and some fine print are a source of sure entertainment, when no one ever begs to see another vacation slide. Something about identity cards is summary—your life on a slab of plastic, a quick-reference tabulation of who you are. I had chosen the Swiss license from my growing collection, leaving its American and British counterparts in their leather slots. Its air of mystery seemed appropriate to my mission. I felt like a spy.

I took an elevator, got off, and proceeded to a glassed-in conference room, where a quartet of long tables had been arranged in a rectangle. I found my name card—COLLINS capitalized in that insistently classificatory French way—and sat down in a chair upholstered in nubby purple fabric. The room began to fill with people: a mustachioed man wearing a tweed blazer, flowered socks, and cat's-eye glasses; a woman in a navy blue pussycat-bow blouse and a hat that looked like a cake. At 9:45 sharp, the chairman called the meeting to order, welcoming the members and guests of the Délégation Générale à la Langue Française's Commission Générale de Terminologie et de Néologie.

The Académie Française, contrary to widespread belief,

does not actually come up with the thousands of new words that ascend to the status of official French every year. Instead, the task falls to the CGTN, a governmental body whose sole purpose is to contrive French replacements for foreign interlopers. (They are almost always English.) The process begins in small committees, where lay experts generate alternatives to whatever terms have recently become popular or necessary in their fields. They make their suggestions to the CGTN, which assesses them and sends them to the Académie Française for a preliminary opinion. The words that survive then undergo a second round of vetting in committee, which culminates in the academy's approval, usually pro forma, upon which the Ministry of Culture and Communication publishes them in an annual report. A constitutional court ruled in 1994 that the state couldn't force private citizens or media organizations to say *façonneur d'image* for "spin doctor," or *beuverie express* instead of "binge drinking," but the terms are binding for public employees. Most languages evolve in a haphazard way. France, however, expends a great deal of money and manpower in an attempt to rationalize the process. Where English is a disinterested capitalist system—may the best word win, be it *bodega* or *feng shui*—French is a proudly *dirigiste* state.

The agenda for the day was the second-round discussion of words relating to the economy and to chemistry.

"We'll start with the list of economic terms," the chairman said, speaking into a small microphone.

The first term, *acteur planétaire*, a calque for "global player," passed without much objection. Next up was *comme si de rien n'était*—literally, "as if nothing was"—which was being proposed as a substitute for "business as usual." The phrase yielded 479,000 hits on Google, excluding mentions, a handout noted in all seriousness, of the album by Men at Work.

"What do we think, members of the General Commission?" the chairman began. "The question we have been asked is to decide whether or not, in all contexts, *comme si rien n'était* is the best translation possible."

Seventeen hands went up.

"*Comme si rien n'était* doesn't seem very flexible," the first speaker said.

"*Comme si rien n'était* is too informal," the man in the fun socks added. "It's not at the same syntactical level as 'business as usual,' nor is it in the same register."

He continued to speak, twirling a nub of a pencil. "We have to find a translation that's more stable, and if we don't, it will become habit in the French language to say 'business as usual.' I worry that the pronunciation for francophones is particularly difficult." He spoke the phrase in English, bombinating the *s*'s like a honeybee on a bloom. "So we have to find something else, and maybe it should be *comme d'habitude*, because that's the exact expression. It's a little more neutral, and a little more likable, and a little more familiar for this type of discourse."

"He's the star of French lexicography," the man on my right whispered. "You know that, right?"

I did not. But I thought that the celebrity lexicographer made a wise point. *Comme si rien n'était* was clunky. Worse, it was literal. It missed the cynicism, the very faint whiff of distrust, that presumably made "business as usual" a favorite idiom of the world of commerce. The point of the phrase, it seemed to me, was that it often implied the perpetuation of an abnormal, or at least unattractive, situation.

Curiously, the committee didn't seem to include many people who had a more than scholastic fluency in English. I was dying to interject, being in possession—merely by birth—of information that others in the room lacked. My national status (I didn't want to look like a rude American) dueled with my linguistic one (French was a language I was going to have to speak). There, in the forge of French language, words were being purpose-built. Was I going to sit by as the committee signed off on faulty prototypes that would soon be flogged to the world's 220 million French speakers?

To watch words get made was to bear witness to an elemental mystery, a moment whose aftermath was as imposing as its origins were supposed to be invisible—the sarsens going up at Stonehenge, the legend taking shape around the campfire. The pedants were also sorcerers, practitioners of a hieratic art. Everything could already be said, but it hadn't been said in the style of their sect, which was why they had to exist. *Comme si rien n'était* was a joke being told for the very first time.

The discussion continued, voices rising. Somebody said that no one even used "business as usual." The next speaker countered that people, especially at big law firms, used it all the time. One woman proposed *dans la continuité*; another liked *sans changement*; another said that since *comme si rien n'était* couldn't be deployed as an adjectival phrase, as "business as usual" often was in English—"a business-as-usual attitude" was the example given—it presented "a singular complication." It didn't occur to the committee members that no one was stopping them from using it as an adjectival phrase if they felt like it. Their extravagant authority coupled with their creative austerity, their reluctance to wield it boldly, seemed to pose as fundamental a French paradox as gorging on foie gras and not getting fat.

. . .

THERE IS A FLAWED YET persistent idea in French, dating to the foundation of the Académie Française, that every word has a single definition, and that every definition corresponds to a single word. The rigorous Cartesian education that is the birthright of the *citoyen* makes itself felt not only in the language but also in the way it's wielded, as though there were no problem that the correct application of logic, the proper progression of steps, cannot solve. Watching the committee trying to bend an English phrase to fit the strictures of French—"If it's not French, it's not clear," they seemed to be saying, inverting Rivarol—I apprehended, at last, the structural underpinnings of the impasses at which Olivier and I often stalled. In English, I was seeking consensus—mirroring Olivier's concerns, wanting to meet in the middle. He was pursuing the right answer, in the conviction that there always was one. If I was performing a close reading, he was solving a proof.

After nearly an hour of debate, the committee was still torn.

"The truth is, in the field of economy I don't see a systematic use of this expression," one of the members admitted.

Someone attempted a last-ditch effort to solidify support for *sans changement.*

"It's a good suggestion, but it would need to be agreed upon by the majority of the members of the commission," the chairman ruled. "I think it is a subject we can revisit. Does everyone agree to move on to other terms?"

Most of the other words passed muster fairly easily. "Hot desking," in a matter of minutes, morphed to *partage de bureau.* "Fun business"—perhaps the Jerry Lewis of economics terms, cherished abroad but ignored at home—was christened *travail amusant.* Straightforwardly enough, "offshoring" became *délocalisation.* But its entourage of spin-offs—"onshoring," "homeshoring," "nearshoring"—gave the committee pause. The working group had suggested that "nearshoring," for example, be rendered *délocalisation dans un pays proche.*

"The question is, what is the definition of 'close'?" one of the members asked. "The concept of 'close' is not very well-defined."

It had been three hours. The committee briefly adjourned. During the break, the man to my right introduced himself. He was Vincent, a linguistics professor from Lyon. His specialty, it turned out, was lexical blending: the formation of words like *fugly* and *spork.*

Every compound or blended word, he explained, demonstrates what is called "headedness"— one of its elements overpowers the other with regard to how the word will be defined. In English, "rightheadedness" prevails: a photosafari is a safari, not a photograph. French generally works the other way around, so that *carburéacteur* (*carburant* + *réacteur*) is jet fuel, rather than a fueled jet.

Maybe this had something to do with why the committee was getting so hung up, why it was unable to see the shores for the nears. French, I felt, didn't need to be able to say "nearshoring." The term existed because it could, because the blocks were there and someone had built it. Why make a plumcot unless you've got a bunch of plums on hand?

When the meeting resumed, we turned to the chemistry terms. *Adiabatique*, *diathermane*, *différence de potentiel électrique de cellule.* I relaxed, letting the words wash over me, a language within a language, once again obscure.

"Madame Collins?" I heard the chairman say.

He was asking for my opinion as to whether *absorption modulée en pression* did justice to the term "pressure swing absorption," a technique for purifying gas.

I straightened my back, tapped my microphone, and looked out at the group.

"Je n'en ai aucune idée," I said, confessing, in irreproachable French, that I hadn't the slightest idea.

OLIVIER SAID TO MEET HIM at the hardware store, the first door on the south after turning east at the light. When I got there, he had already bought what he needed. It was raining, nearly time for lunch. We walked a few blocks and ducked into an indoor market. The northern aisle was full of vendors: a butcher; a *charcutier*; a fishmonger, his wares laid out on ice. We stopped and called to the southwest side of the counter, where he was filleting a perch.

"Five hundred grams of smoked salmon, please?"

"Ça fait vingt-trois quarante," the fishmonger yelled back, indicating that the order would be twenty-three francs and forty centimes.

Olivier extracted two twenties and a five-franc coin from the ziplock bag that served as his wallet.

"Pretty sure he said *vingt-trois quarante*," I said.

"It's *trente-trois quarante*," Olivier replied, handing over the cash.

The fishmonger counted the money and pushed one of the twenties back over the counter.

"Did I just school you in French?" I blurted out, my American-volume gloat turning the heads of Saturday-morning matrons, with their bouffants and little pushcarts.

My sense of satisfaction was short-lived.

"Yeah," Olivier admitted, before reminding me, "Because I'm deaf in my west ear."

That, at least, is how the story might go in Guugu Yimithirr, a language spoken by about a thousand people in Far North Queensland, the province that sticks up like a cowlick from the crown of Australia's coast. Captain Cook made the first written record of Guugu Yimithirr after his ship, the *Endeavor*, ran aground on the Great Barrier Reef in June 1770, stranding him and his crew for several months at the mouth of what is now the Endeavor River.

On the morning of July 23, Cook sent some men out into the countryside to gather greens. One of them, he recalled in his diary, "stragled from the rest, and met with 4 of the Natives by a fire," on which they were broiling a fowl and the hind leg of a turtle. The man went and sat with them. After a while, Cook wrote, "they suffer'd him to go away without offering the least insult, and perceiving that he did not go right for the Ship they directed him which way to go." What is incidental in Cook would resurface, two centuries later, as a critical linguistic discovery: speakers of Guugu Yimithirr, orienting themselves exclusively via the cardinal directions, possess exceptional spatial skills.

Languages can encode space in three ways: geocentrically, in which the frame of reference is fixed ("I am south of the fire"); intrinsically, in which the frame of reference depends on an object ("I am behind the fire"); and egocentrically, in which the frame of reference aligns with the viewer ("I am to the left of the fire"). Most languages make use of at least two of them. English avails itself of all three, so that an English speaker can say, "Walk south on Main Street, continue in front of the library, and turn right into the park." Guugu Yimithirr, however, is among a handful of languages that offer only the geocentric option. It requires every speaker, whenever he wants to communicate the slightest fact about location, which is to say basically anytime he wants to communicate anything at all, to place himself on a grid. Studies of Guugu Yimithirr speakers have shown that their senses of direction are more or less unshakable. Plunk one down in heavy fog, turn him loose in a forest, shut him up in a windowless room, lead him into a cave—he'll still be able to position himself as truly as if he were following a GPS. Several decades after the fact, an elderly man recounted to a researcher his experience of getting caught in a storm, capsizing his boat, and having to swim several miles to the shore. The sharks that menaced him, he recalled, were swimming north.

The existence of Guugu Yimithirr is among the most persuasive exhibits for the argument that language influences culture. By forcing its speakers to constantly articulate their whereabouts, it effectively turns their brains into compasses. Linguistic universalists have objected strenuously to this conclusion, contending that it confuses causation with correlation—John McWhorter writes that it's akin to saying "Tribes with no words for clothing do not wear clothes." They dismiss the superb navigational abilities displayed by speakers of Guugu Yimithirr as a function of their environment: if you live on flat land in the bush, without many landmarks, it makes sense that you would rely on cardinal directions. But plenty of people who live in similar environments use egocentric orienteering systems. And children are able to master geocentric ones at an early age, before they've had much exposure to any landscape but the lap and the crib.

Guy Deutscher explains that, while English speakers perceive two hotel rooms across a hall from each other as exact replicas (both bathroom doors on the left, the vanity behind them, the soap on the left-hand ledge), speakers of Guugu Yimithirr experience them as diametrically reversed (everything turned north-side-south). "Does this all mean that we and speakers of Guugu Yimithirr sometimes remember 'the same reality' differently?" he asks. Guugu Yimithirr, he concludes, "must be a crucial factor in bringing about the perfect pitch for directions and the corresponding patterns of memory that seem so weird and unattainable to us."

One way to settle the debate, once and for all, would be to raise a bunch of Los Angelenos or Tokyoites from birth in Guugu Yimithirr. That is not going to happen, for ethical and practical reasons. But a number of experiments devised in recent years have illustrated the connection between features of languages and the different ways that their speakers behave. Taken in the aggregate, the work of the neo-Whorfians, as they're known, suggests that language can shape culture, rather than merely reflecting it, resurrecting the reputation of their namesake from the pauper's grave in which Chomsky laid it.

It was a Sunday afternoon, hot and still. In the summer, most cities swell with bandstands and fruit carts and air-conditioner window units, dripping on the brims of the baseball caps of packs of tourists. But Geneva felt drained in a way that suggested swift evacuation, as though someone had just pulled the plug of a bathtub, leaving behind a few damp, tottering toys.

I went to the park. Not much was happening: a retiree practiced tai chi; some teenagers wafted pot smoke and Swiss rap. (The leading Swiss rapper, Stress, had a business degree and was a former employee of Procter & Gamble. "Switzerland, Switzerland, mais qu'est-ce qui se passe," went the refrain of his hit song "Fuck Blocher," which protested the election of the industrialist Christoph Blocher to the Swiss Federal Council.) Spotting a wide patch of grass, I pitched my canvas chair near a footpath. It squired pedestrians under oaks and past rhododendrons toward the granite eminences of the Reformation Wall: a sixteen-foot-tall John Calvin, Roger Williams in a cockel hat.

I sat down and tipped off my shoes, crossing my legs at the knees, so that the top one formed a little shelf, my foot dangling off. I had a cold bottle of water and *Bonjour Tristesse*, Françoise Sagan's novel of estival ennui. It was peaceful, if nothing else. "He was following the coast in a little sailboat and keeled over in front of our creek," I read. "I helped him get his things together and, amid our laughs, I learned that his name was Cyril, that he was a law student spending his vacation with his mother in a neighboring villa." The Mediterranean seemed very far away.

I was just getting into Cyril—"He had a Latin face, very brown, very open, with something stable, something protective, that pleased me"—when I noticed a less alluring character—he had red shorts and flip-flops—walking in the direction of the grass. I went back to reading, underlining the words I didn't know. *L'étourdissement*—dizziness. *Les soupirs*—sighs. The man continued on the footpath until it delivered him just a few inches in front of where I was sitting. Before I knew what was happening, he had reached out and grabbed my foot. He was squeezing it, like a lemon.

I was dumbfounded. The man walked on, unscolded, as I

tried to formulate a riposte. I could hear the curses, but they were just beyond reach. I felt as though I were trawling around the bottom of a messy purse for a missing set of keys.

According to tradecraft, a person will always reveal his native language at the moment of orgasm. This was very much the opposite situation. I was unnerved both by the bizarreness of the incident and by the fact that I hadn't, in the heat of the moment, instinctively blurted out some expression of my disgust. The afternoon curdled, I trudged back to the apartment, conjuring up the insults I would scream, the remonstrances I would let rain, the next time a stranger touched my foot.

Later, I would look back on that day almost with fondness. I hadn't known to whom I was speaking, and thus how to speak. Taken by surprise, I was unable to decide whether my primary audience was my assailant, the public, or myself. My silence, I realized, hadn't sprung from a deficit. I'd been paralyzed not by a lack of options, a dearth of language, but by an embarrassment of them.

THE STATUE OF LIBERTY HAS a rosebud mouth and taut breasts. Why is she a woman? Inspired by her knowledge of gendered nouns in her native Russian, Lera Boroditsky, a cognitive scientist at the University of California, San Diego, analyzed 765 artworks—personifying such abstract concepts as justice, time, and love—created since 1200 by French, German, Italian, and Spanish artists. She found that 78 percent of the time, the gender of the figure matched its grammatical gender in the artist's native language. Liberty, in other words, is likely to be a woman when it corresponds to a feminine noun, *la liberté*, and its creator is French. Boroditsky summarized the phenomenon as "grammar quite literally carved in stone." She and her collaborator acknowledged that they hadn't proved causation, but even in cases for which the cultural precedent was weak, there was a strong correlation between the gender of a word and its representation. In Laurent de La Hyre's *Allégorie de la géométrie*, math is a raven-tressed babe.

In recent years, neo-Whorfian researchers have begun to chip away at Chomsky's universal grammar, redeeming some of linguistic relativism's less outlandish ideas. "Is anybody born with the concept of a carburetor, or a bureaucrat?" Boroditsky asks. In another test, she instructed speakers of German and Spanish to think about a bridge—*die Brücke*, a feminine noun, in the former and *el puente*, a masculine one, in the latter—and to describe it in three adjectives. The Germans tended to use stereotypically feminine words such as *beautiful*, *fragile*, and *elegant*, while the Spanish favored masculine ones such as *sturdy*, *towering*, and *strong*. Boroditsky then created a nonsense language called Gumbuzi, in which all nouns were either "oosative" (indicated by the prefix *oos-*) or "soupative" (indicated by the prefix *sou-*), and taught it to native English speakers. The oosative/soupative distinction extended to both living beings—males fell into one category; females into the other—and inanimate objects. Half of Boroditsky's subjects learned that pots, pens, spoons, giants, and boys were oosative and that pans, forks, ballerinas, and pencils were soupative, while the other half learned exactly the opposite. The former group, when quizzed, described the first set of objects as masculine and the second as feminine, while the latter group did the reverse. After only twenty minutes of speaking Gumbuzi, they were demonstrating Whorfian effects.

The neo-Whorfians make a compelling case in the field of color. In 1858 William Gladstone noticed that there was something off in Homer's depiction of the natural world. Why, he wondered, had Homer described blood as black? Why were oxen and the sea alike "wine-dark"? Why had he failed entirely to mention the color of the sky? The Greeks, he determined, must have seen color in a quantitatively different way. His theory set off a century of inquiry into the naturalness, or lack thereof, of categories of color. Some of his followers concluded that the Greeks must have been color-blind. Some researchers accepted eyesight as an explanation for perceptual differences; others argued that everyone's vision was equal and that the muted palettes of Homer and other "primitive peoples" were a result of vague vocabularies. The idea that the rainbow might be arbitrarily constructed by language—that each language, working with the same spectrum, might divide it into different stripes—enjoyed a vogue during the heyday of the Sapir-Whorf hypothesis, but soon faded. In 1969 Brent Berlin and Paul Kay proposed their basic color theory, which held that, as languages evolve, they add color terms in a predictable sequence of seven stages, beginning with dark and light and culminating in the acquisition of purple, pink, orange, and gray.

Berlin and Kay's theory entered into dogma, but although it was supposedly universal, it was based on a culturally specific assumption that color was a natural property of the physical world. As Aneta Pavlenko explains, some languages—Bellonese, Mursi, Pirahã, Warlpiri, Kalam, Yélî Dnye—"do not encode color as an abstract dimension independent of other properties of material objects." Instead they focus on other characteristics, assimilating hue into distinctions of pattern, ripeness, brightness, translucence, humidity, shape, or location. A banana might be "ripe" but not "yellow," even if yellow is implied in its ripeness. When asked by scientists to identify color samples, Mursi speakers, unsure of their responses, said not "I don't know the name of that color" but "There's no such beast." In *The Bilingual Mind*, Pavlenko makes a breathtaking argument: "These distinct outcomes suggest that categorical perception of colors, cups, and cattle—and, for that matter, snow and ice—is shaped by our engagement with the material world, with lexical categories serving as a means of focusing selective attention on the relevant distinctions." Perhaps the stubborn belief of her overwhelmingly white, male, English-speaking colleagues in the naturalness of such categories, she suggests, is a Whorfian effect in itself.

In 2007 scientists from Stanford, MIT, and UCLA asked Russian and English speakers to sit in front of a computer screen, on which they presented various pictures of three squares. In each picture the squares were arranged in a triangle: one on top, the remaining pair below. They were all blue, spanning twenty gradations from what an English speaker would probably describe as robin's-egg blue to a midnight shade. The color of one of the bottom squares always matched the top square, while the other bottom square was a different shade. The scientists instructed the subjects to hit a button as soon as they could identify the matching pair.

In Russian, you can't call the sky "blue." The language obliges its speakers to make a distinction between *siniy* (dark blue) and *goluboy* (light blue), so that what is in English one color becomes in Russian two. This is the sort of quirk that dinner-party linguists love to muse about, but the researchers were able to measure its effect on visual perception in an objective way. Russian speakers, they found, could distinguish between dark and light shades of blue 10 percent faster than English speakers. (Universalists will point out that the difference is only 124 milliseconds, in the course of making an argument that typically proceeds from "There are no Whorfian effects" to "Okay, there are, but they're really small.") To test whether this edge was due to language, the researchers then asked the subjects to perform the same exercise while memorizing an eight-digit number. With their language processing disrupted, Russian speakers were no better at the color-sorting task than their English peers. The color of the sea depends, to some extent, on the language we speak.

Every language, we know, has its blind spots—until recently, there were no crustaceans in emoji, other than the fried shrimp. But emojis constitute a surprisingly eloquent new language. They seem not only to articulate feelings but also to create them—hundreds of previously unregistered microsentiments. Emojis are, of course, pictograms. And while scientists might dismiss an argument for their uniqueness as the latest variant of the Eskimo problem, those who use them can testify to their strange expressive heft. Sometimes I scan the rows of characters looking for the emotion I want to get across, rather than the other way around. There's the winged bundle of money, blameless as an angel, that can make you believe a splurge was preordained. The sulky pumpkin, the jocose ghost. There is no word for "bashful face with pinkening cheeks that obliquely suggest I'm both embarrassed and pleased." You just have to send a text.

"Do you see things if you don't know what they are?" Geoff Dyer asks. You can, but the carved edge of a table seems more conspicuous once you know it's gadrooning, a pouchy cloud more memorable once you can call it a mammatus. This is why technical vocabularies develop. It's why, according to researchers, Mandarin—which has eleven basic number names versus more than two dozen in English ("eleven," for example, is "ten-one")—may be a better language for learning math. Such is the power of language in the perception of identity that a group of English-speaking white children told researchers that they thought themselves more likely to grow up to be English-speaking black people than white people who spoke French. Maybe the best metaphor for Whorfian effects is predictive texting. Even if the prefabricated chunks of expression can be overridden with a bit of effort, we often choose to accept them.

BILINGUALS OVERWHELMINGLY report that they feel like different people in different languages. They do so for a multitude of reasons, some of which are less attributable to any language in particular than to having a new language itself. A person may be a loan shark in his new language when he was an ophthalmologist in his native tongue. Perhaps he spoke Polish to his first wife but speaks Portuguese with the second. He may have scaled or slid down the ladder of class. He may have changed his politics, or his name. During the transition from one language to another, people undergo deaths, births, traumas, triumphs, displacements, adjustments, and the simple fact of aging.

One Saturday morning Olivier and I woke up early, packed overnight bags, and got into the car. We were driving to the mountains to see Hugo, who was there on a ski trip during his winter break. He and Marie and two of his friends were staying in a one-bedroom condo, so we'd booked a hotel room for the night. Olivier started up the car and typed the hotel's name into Google, intending to enter the address into the GPS.

"Putain," he said. "It's saying that Hotel le Montana is in Chamonix."

This was odd. Chamonix was two hours north of La Tania, the village in the southeast of France where Olivier's family had been going to ski since he was a kid.

I entered "hotel montana la tania" into my phone. The same listing for the Hotel le Montana in Chamonix popped up.

Olivier dialed the number. We had in fact booked a nonrefundable room for the night in the entirely wrong village.

We couldn't figure out what had happened, why the Hotel le Montana in La Tania—one of the few accommodations in town—had disappeared from view. But we didn't have time to stick around and sort things out, knowing that it was *le chassé croisé*—the designated changeover day for French vacationers, who, as orthodox in their holiday schedules as their lunch hours, traditionally hand in their rental keys and descend upon the nation's autoroutes at exactly the same moment, causing traffic jams as dense and reliable as the steps of a quadrille, from which the phrase comes. Despite not having a place to stay, we pulled out of the parking lot and headed toward La Tania.

Apartment blocks flattened into farmland, and I Googled. Grass gave way to rock and I Googled some more. Everywhere I called, the answer was the same: no vacancy. I expanded my search to the surrounding area, hoping that, of the millions of French people traveling that day, at least one of them must have also committed some logistical screwup, freeing a room for us.

I dialed a guesthouse with a website decked in edelweiss.

"Hello?" the man who picked up said.

"Hi, I'm wondering if you have a room for tonight?"

"You'd have had to have booked it months ago," he replied, his English accent becoming clear. "You do know it's half term for the UK, and the rest of the world?"

"I asked for a room, not a lecture," I said, pressing the red button as I lamented one of the great downsides of the digital age, the extinction of the flamboyant hang-up.

"Quel con," Olivier grumbled.

When we got to La Tania, we parked the car and set out on foot to investigate the situation. Passing by a *traiteur* (offering both *blanquette de veau* and English breakfast sausages), ski rental shops, a pub, and a tent under which the tourist authority was ladling out free cups of Chartreuse-spiked *chocolat chaud*, we followed the village's only road to the Hotel le Montana. It was indeed still standing. We walked in, knocking the sludge from our boots. A rugby game was playing on a number of flat-screen TVs.

"Bonjour, Mademoiselle," Olivier said to the woman sitting behind the reception desk.

She squinted at him. "Do you speak English?"

"Non."

The woman looked distressed. She was barely twenty—a chalet girl in a polo shirt, clearly out of her depth—but Olivier was unmoved. We waited as she went to fetch someone.

Another young woman appeared. Olivier asked whether it was possible to book a room, refusing to rescue her as she tried to explain, in tortured French, that the hotel no longer took independent bookings and was now exclusively dedicated to housing the participants of package tours. Olivier was normally polite to a fault. I'd rarely seen him so belligerent. I found his fight sort of amusing, even though the gambit left me muted, in danger of giving up the game whatever language I picked. I understood then why people insist on different languages, even if they can say the same thing equally well in more than one of them. The integrity of Olivier's memories—of the twelve-hour car rides from Bordeaux; of his family milieu; of his first taste of freedom, flying past his parents on squeaking powder—depended on the persistence of the medium through which they were formed. He needed to speak

French in La Tania, and for La Tania to speak French to him, to be who he'd always been there.

It is often assumed that the mother tongue is the language of the true self. And in many ways it remains the primal vehicle, the first and most effective responder in moments of celebration or crisis. A person who has spoken English most of her life is always going to speak English when she stubs her toe. But if first languages are reservoirs of emotion, second languages can be rivers undammed. A Swiss friend who speaks Spanish with her parents and siblings and French with her husband and children told me that she feels a certain freedom in English, where she occupies the role of neither sister nor mother. People are more likely to say they'd push a man off a bridge—in order to save five other people, about to be hit by a train—when the dilemma is presented in their second language. Scientists call this the emancipatory detachment effect.

For me, French—though it could have been Arabic or Swahili—was a reprieve from the relentless prerogative of individualism. The crazy thing about learning a language is that once you've internalized the vocabulary, you have to figure out how it goes together—according to Steven Pinker, in a language with 60,000 words, there are approximately 100 million trillion ten-word sentences that make grammatical sense. Knowing which permutations work is, to some extent, intuitive. But fluency is also a function of familiarity, as grammar offers few clues as to the parts of speech that are not so much idioms as loose affinities. How is one to know that *inclement* almost always goes with *weather*; that aspersions are cast but insults hurled; that observers are keen; that processions are orderly; that—as someone apparently decreed sometime in the early years of this century—e-mails must be shot and drinks grabbed? In English, I strained to avoid such formulations. But in French, conformity was my goal. Speaking offered a sense of community, the rare chance to crowd-source my personal thesaurus. I was trying to join in, not to distinguish myself. It was such a happy thing to strive for cliché.

I had my pet words. *Rocambolesque*: extraordinary, fantastical. *Bled*: one's village, an almost genealogical "hometown," borrowed from the Arabic. *Se debrouiller*, with its mess of vowels, suggested resourcefulness far more strongly to me than its trig English counterpart, "to manage." "Gerrymandering" was *charcutage*—as in *charcuterie*—*electoral*, the lexical calf of the irregularly carved French cow. More than that, I began to warm to the strictures of French, the elegance of its form. When I spoke English, I desperately missed the subjunctive, which could lift a confusingly flat eventuality into a far more delicate realm. With thousands of repetitions, *vous* versus *tu* and the concatenations that they set into motion begin to feel like a secular catechism, its recitation both comforting and sublime. The correctness that French requires revealed itself as not vanity but courtesy, guaranteeing that every person, however weak or humble, commanded a measure of respect. So much could be conveyed with so little.

The sangfroid of French was beginning to seep into my English. "I got my ticket!" I told Olivier. "Sorry, sorry, *the* ticket."

A month later I flew to New York. In the immigration line at JFK, I stood behind a dazed older man.

"Who are you?" the Homeland Security officer bellowed when he fumbled to produce his passport. The undifferentiated English "you" hit me like a bludgeon. Whatever had regenerated in its place felt twice as dexterous.

On the plane I had read about a barber taken hostage in Paris, and felt a surge of darkly amused pride.

"I'm going to be sixty-five the 22nd of December, I'm about to retire, I don't want to die with a bullet to the head!" he'd told his captors, according to the news report. "Also, I would prefer that we didn't *tutoyer* each other, given my age."

BERTHA PAPPENHEIM INVENTED the phrase "the talking cure." The daughter of a wealthy grain trader, Pappenheim—her doctor, Josef Breuer, gave her the pseudonym Anna O.—had received the typical education of a Viennese bourgeoise, with instruction in religion, piano, horseback riding, and foreign languages. She was possessed, Breuer wrote, of "a powerful intellect" and "an astonishingly quick grasp of things and penetrating intuition." When she was sixteen, her parents pulled her out of school. It could not have been easy for her, watching her brother continue his studies while she passed her days doing little but needlework and helping her mother prepare kosher meals.

In July 1880, when Pappenheim was twenty-one, her father contracted quinsy, a complication of tonsillitis. She devoted herself to caring for him, neglecting her own health. In December she took to bed, complaining of headaches, impaired vision, paresis of the legs, arms, and neck. The walls of the room, she said, looked as though they were caving in. According to Breuer, she alternated between two mental states. In one, she was melancholy. In the other, she threw cushions at people, shredded her bedclothes, and suffered hallucinations of black snakes.

Pappenheim's most unusual symptoms occurred in the realm of language. In her agitated periods—Breuer called them *absences*, using the French—"she used then to stop in the middle of a sentence, repeat her last words, and after a short pause go on talking." In the afternoons, she became catatonic. An hour after sunset she would wake up, repeating the words "tormenting, tormenting," but otherwise hardly able to speak. Eking out fragments of the six languages she knew—German, Hebrew, Yiddish, French, Italian, and English—she made little sense. "Later she lost her command of grammar and syntax; she no longer conjugated verbs, and eventually she used only infinitives, for the most part she omitted both the definite and the indefinite article," Breuer wrote. Postulating that her sickness was a suppression, that some great upset had induced her inarticulateness, he encouraged her to discuss it. Doing so, she regained movement in the left side of her body, and her paraphasia receded. She appeared to understand German, "but thenceforward she spoke only in English—apparently, however, without knowing she was doing so."

On April 1, Pappenheim got out of bed. On April 5, her father died. For the better part of a year, she refused nourishment, subsisting on melons. She demonstrated a particular distaste for bread. Now she read French and Italian, but didn't recognize German. She continued to speak only in English, becoming "so deaf" that Breuer had to pass her notes. Even her penmanship changed. She wrote with her left hand in the style of Roman printed letters, copying the alphabet from her volumes of Shakespeare.

"I used to visit her in the evening, when I knew I should find her in her hypnosis," Breuer wrote, "and I then relieved her of the whole stock of imaginative products which she had accumulated since my last visit." The cycle persisted: by day Pappenheim built up anxieties, which she and Breuer "worked off" by night, until they had made it through the entire back catalog of her distress. Gradually her condition improved. On her last day of treatment, in July 1882, Breuer arranged the furniture to resemble her father's sickroom and had her act out the hallucination that had "constituted the root of her whole illness," in which she had watched, stricken, as a snake attacked him while he slept. The horror subsided only when Pappenheim heard the whistle of a train. In the original scene, she had been able to think and pray only in English, but, when she reenacted it, her German came back. "After this she left Vienna and travelled for a while, but it was a considerable time before she regained her mental balance entirely," Breuer wrote. "Since then she has enjoyed complete health."

Pappenheim also called the talking cure "chimney-sweeping." When I read this, I understood why she might have wanted to speak English rather than German, why, in the intensity of her feeling, she chose, consciously or not, to reject her mother (and father) tongue. Freud, lecturing later about her case, asserted, "Almost all of the symptoms had arisen in this way as residues—'precipitates' they might be called—of emotional experiences." A fresh language can be a solvent to heartache. Perhaps speaking English was, for Pappenheim, another form of chimney-sweeping—a way to self-medicate, a purification ritual, a brushing away of a stultifying late adolescence, the family milieu, Vater Pappenheim's stories about grain. German was bread. English was melons. Something about it must have made her feel clean.

In French, it is difficult to be excited in a nonsexual way. One can *avoir hâte* of something, or be eager to do it. Or something can *tarder* one, and make one impatient. It's feasible to be *enthousiaste* or *agité*, but to be *excité* almost demands a physical stimulus.

It was hard for me to tamp down my enthusiasm. Once I'd consigned excitement to the erotic realm, the word I missed most was *fun*—another adjective that I sent floating into the atmosphere as lightly as though I were blowing bubbles. Dozens of times a day, I bumped up against the absence of the two words, until my need for them came to seem an overreliance. English, it should be said, is not a homogeneous entity. Like every language, it comprises multitudes, Indian English and South African English being no more or no less Englishes than the English of the Queen. The baseline register of my English—the English of an educated, coastal-dwelling white American—sounded like exaggeration. I started to feel as though I'd spent most of my life speaking in all caps.

The linguist Dan Jurafsky writes of a phenomenon called "semantic bleaching," in which words, most often in the affective realm, lose their power over time, so that the "awe" fades from "awesome" and "horrible" becomes merely unpleasant. French, for me, was semantic baking soda, reinvigorating my expressive palette. I realized how many fun things I was excit edly calling "the best" once it became clear that the formulation didn't really work in French, because French speakers took it literally. Tell a francophone, "This is the best *tarte au citron*!" and it will come across less as sincere praise than an asininity. She'll go silent as she tries to figure out what you're comparing it to, whether you've actually sampled all the *tartes au citron* the world has to offer. It was hard to accept that, in French, a compliment resonated in inverse proportion to the force with which it was offered. Much better to say the tart is *bonne* than *très bonne*. Discrimination was a higher virtue than effusiveness.

In Francesca Marciano's novel *Rules of the Wild*, the

narrator—an Italian woman living in Kenya with a safari operator of Scottish origin—admits that speaking in English obliges her to be "simpler, less Machiavellian." In French, I experienced the opposite sensation. Its austerity made me feel more complicated. I was aware of my wiles—of the consequences of excitement—in a way that abjured innocence. James Baldwin described French as "that curiously measured and vehement language, which sometimes reminds me of stiffening egg white and sometimes of stringed instruments but always of the underside and aftermath of passion." I liked how he captured the relationship between the obliqueness of French—the under and the after—and its erotic charge. The formality of the language, paradoxically, heightened its potential for feeling. Shedding superlatives, I felt as though I were enacting a linguistic version of Coco Chanel's dictum that before leaving the house, a woman should stop, look in the mirror, and remove one piece of jewelry.

Men and women were both more distinct and less adversarial. This wasn't just the language; it was the culture that went along with it, the interplay of gendered adjectives and sexual politics, standards of beauty and courtesy titles that rendered me Madame Collins, not Lauren. The slack filial rapport between American men and women—even those who are romantically involved—didn't seem like a possibility. Neither did the brand of resentment that accompanies the melding of roles, the confusion over who's supposed to do what when. I had to laugh when I read, on the French state department's website, a warning to travelers to the United States: "It is recommended to adopt a reserved attitude toward members of the opposite sex. Some comments, attitudes, or jokes, anodyne in Latin countries, can lead to prosecution."

Browsing the Internet one day, I came across a powerful American executive's Twitter bio. The third line—"wife of awesome guy"—struck me as too much and too little, overdone and neutered at the same time. My English self sometimes longed for uncomplicated American manhood. When, one afternoon in Geneva, I saw a freshly showered man in khakis and a chamois shirt tossing damp bangs out of his eyes, probably smelling of Old Spice, I almost chased him down the street, just to hear him say "hi." My French self thought, Who calls their husband an "awesome guy"?

French is said to be the language of love, meaning seduction. I was uncovering in it an etiquette for loving, what happens next. My acquisition of the language had been a sort of conversion, and in the same way that Catholics value the Latin mass for its grandeur, French represented to me a sacred ritual. I had once interpreted Olivier's reticence as pessimism, but I now saw the deep romanticism, the hopefulness, of not wanting to overstate or to overpromise. *Vous* and *tu* concentrated intimacy by dividing it into distinct shades—the emotional equivalent of two shades of blue. I understood, finally, why it made Olivier happy when I wore makeup; why he didn't call me his best friend; why I had never heard him burp. Love was not fusion. *Je t'aime* was enough.

WE WERE IN THE KITCHEN one night, talking about taking a vacation. We hadn't been on one in a long time. I was pushing for two weeks.

"It might be tricky to ask for more than one," Olivier said. "I think it's better if I take them separately."

"But it doesn't really make any sense to take one now and

another later," I said. "It's the same amount of time, and it'll just seem like you're gone more."

Olivier fixed me with a stare.

"What's your argument?" he said.

The word *argument* was a self-fulfilling prophecy. I thought I had just made one. I was upset that we couldn't have a conversation about a vacation without it turning into an adversarial process, a trial with a winner and a loser. Olivier was always prosecuting me on form, pushing me to be more precise, haranguing me about changing the subject. His fixation on clarity drove me crazy: I found his queries unanswerable, and besides, I didn't want to drink piña coladas with a member of the Délégation Générale à la Langue Française.

"Why does everything have to be one?" I said. I could feel the tears rising like a tide, the silvery ache in my throat.

"I just made a poor choice of word," he countered. "How would you like it if I did that to you in French?"

I decided to try something different, an alternate route around the old dead end.

"Bon," I said, taking him up on the challenge. "Donc, parlons!"

We went back and forth, him accusing me of not explaining myself straightforwardly, me accusing him of creating a hostile atmosphere. I acquitted myself surprisingly confidently, the need to concentrate negating the luxury of fear.

"Si tu veux savoir mes pensées, tu devrais essayer à faire une ambiance qui les élicite," I said, relishing the severity of my French persona, the sibilant regimented syllables that seemed to carry within them not the slightest hint of doubt.

"C'est 'solliciter,' pas 'éliciter,'" Olivier replied, before he could stop himself from pointing out that I'd spat out a nonexistent cognate.

. . .

It felt good to touch Olivier in his own language—to be able to push his buttons, graze his pleasure points. I was secretly flattered that he considered my French of a high enough caliber to be correctable. We could grapple bare-handed. But I sometimes worried that I had traded in the gloves for a mask.

The ancient Greek word for acting is *hypokrisis.* Aristotle used it in *On Rhetoric* to refer to an orator's method of delivery, writing that the style of a speech is as important as the content. There is a thread that runs directly from performance to speech to hypocrisy, in the contemporary sense of pretending to a character or an attitude—a voice—that one doesn't actually possess.

"It is our contention that second-language learning in all of its dimensions exerts a very specific demand with regard to self-representation," the authors of a study wrote. "Essentially, to learn a second language is to take on a new identity." They had asked eighty-seven students at the University of Michigan to drink a cocktail, which they served in a stemmed glass, garnished with a cherry and a twist of lemon. Each drink contained between zero and three ounces of ninety-proof liquor (cognac, light and dark rum). The students, English speakers, were then asked to pronounce a sequence of words in Thai. Those who had consumed an ounce and a half of alcohol scored better than the teetotalers; the two- and three-ounce drinkers performed worse. Small amounts of alcohol, the researchers wrote, lowered the subjects' inhibitions, "inducing a state of greater permeability of ego boundaries." Language skills, they concluded, "are related to basic differences in the flexibility of psychic processes." The religious authorities were right to perceive the relationship between foreign languages and a certain fungibility of the soul. To speak one well, you have to be either Bradley Cooper or drunk.

It was hard for me to discern where the line between adaptation and dissimulation lay. I wanted to be flexible, but I didn't want to be spineless, or to stretch myself into impotence, like the object of the Afrikaans pejorative *soutpiel*, with one foot in Europe and one foot in Africa, and a "salt penis" in between. I wanted to join the party, but I didn't want to be a guest at a costume ball, a Jamesian courtier "marrying foreigners, forming artificial tastes." I wanted to speak French and to sound like North Carolina. I was hoping, though I didn't know whether it was possible, to have become a different person without having changed.

Six

THE SUBJUNCTIVE
Le Subjonctif

THE *MEGA SMERELDA* hoisted her stern doors and we drove into the loading deck, where attendants in yellow jumpsuits were stacking cars as though they were stuffing suitcases into a thirty-three-ton trunk. It was almost midnight. Out on the tarmac, a delay had incited an open-air picnic—families passing around gallons of juice, kids dipping fingers into vats of Nutella, husbands waiting for half an hour at an overwhelmed snack truck to procure foot-long hot dogs for wives who never would have eaten them otherwise, as sea spray and gas fumes and feet sticking out of rolled-down windows mingled in the steaming August night. We got out of the car and took the stairs up to the reception desk. There was a spaghetteria and casino carpet, gold banisters and fluorescent blue cocktails garnished with pineapple wedges. The air smelled fried. Part of me wanted to power through and join the party, but we got our key and went straight to the cabin. I had been starving; now I was luxuriantly tired. Olivier pushed aside the curtains and we stared out at the sea, fuzzed with Toulon's receding lights.

We slept tangled up in a narrow bed with hospital corners and a pilled yellow blanket. After what seemed like minutes, an intercom crackled.

"Bonjour, mesdames et messieurs. Il est six heures quarante-cinq et le temps est beau."

It was 6:45 a.m. The weather was good. I got up and looked out the window. An egg crate of hills coddled the harbor. We had arrived in Bastia.

It was my second time on Corsica, the pinecone-shaped island that hangs between the coasts of France and Italy, its stem sticking up into the Ligurian Sea. The summer before, Violeta and Teddy had rented a house there, putting down money months earlier to secure the best deal. They had invited Fabrice and his girlfriend, Anne-Laure, and Olivier and me. We'd all booked flights. When July rolled around, Olivier hadn't been able to get away from work. It was somehow determined that I'd go to Corsica solo, as a sort of household delegate.

Initially, I was not thrilled about this assignment. In the end I had enjoyed myself so much—as a fifth wheel (the French, disturbingly, is *tenir la chandelle*, "to hold the candle"), in a language I could barely speak—that we'd decided to return. The best day of my year had been the one on which we'd gotten a boat and followed the frills of the island's northeastern coast, jumping overboard into jade water that looked as though it would shatter. Fabrice had taken a picture that day of Anne-Laure, Violeta, Teddy, and me, our heads bobbing like buoys in a swimming hole buttressed by limestone cliffs as high as the walls of a cathedral. For twelve months it had served as my phone's wallpaper. The home screen was set to an image I'd once have found unthinkably saccharine. I'd taken it when we'd stopped for a glass of wine in a hilltop town full of stray cats. Every time I swiped a thumb over it, it made me happy: the word *L'amour*, scrawled, in a hand that looked strangely like my own, on a wall the color of calamine lotion.

We exited the ferry and drove south. Cork oaks, dense as heads of broccoli, sprouted from the fields. The *maquis* was a fleece of arbutus and myrtle, sage and juniper, broom and lentisk. Bastia to Aléria to La Testa to Olmuccio to Muchietti Bianchi—the villages were barely intersections now—to the big tree, where we took a right.

A Dutch caretaker let us into the house, which belonged to a Parisian businessman who, judging from the bric-a-brac on display, liked a round of golf. The place was perfect. We were relieved. In the lonely depths of the Swiss winter, a week in a hot climate surrounded by all of our relatives had seemed like a great idea. We hadn't been sure who would show up: Violeta and Teddy were *juilletistes* (there is actually a French word for those who take their vacations in July, as opposed to August); my father, intrepid in his youth, now hated to travel, though we had been hoping to lure him with the opportunity to visit the birthplace of Napoleon (who spoke French with a Corsican accent his entire life). We'd invited the twelve members of our combined families to join us. To our surprise, they had all accepted.

"C'est pas mal," Olivier said. He was pacing the house, opening shutters and testing out mattresses, trying to figure out whom we should assign to sleep where.

I was filling the refrigerator with the load we'd carried from Geneva—on one side bottles of rosé and Pellegrino, the other Coronas and cans of Diet Coke, squaring off like toy soldiers.

Our families had met once before, at our wedding. To make the most of being in Europe, Matt and his wife, Melissa—like him a lawyer in Wilmington—had added a weekend in Paris to their trip. My brother, experiencing the gastronomy of France for the first time, had been inspired to compose a few verses: "They call me the *fromagerie* / 'cause I cut the cheese," went one. Olivier's relatives, who called the language I spoke "American," weren't particularly well versed in our culture either. Still, a tentative bond had taken hold between our two families. They seemed to consider each other long-lost members of the same tribe, as though the language gap were a fissure that had just opened up one day, on ground that they already held in common.

In the months leading up to the trip, tidings of goodwill had pinged back and forth.

"Dear Lauren, this 6th of June we take measure of all the aid brought by your country for our liberation," Teddy, born in 1936, wrote to me on the sixtieth anniversary of the Normandy landings. "Of course, we know it, but it's very moving, and I wanted to tell you that we think of all who died for our freedom. Please share our emotion with your parents."

My mother, in anticipation of the trip, had bought some Instant Immersion French software at Costco. She'd been listening to it every morning on her speed walk up and down the road. For someone who hadn't spoken French since high school, her progress was impressive.

"Voici mon mot du jour que me fait rire"—Here, my word of the day that made me laugh—read the subject line of an e-mail I received from her one afternoon. I opened up the message, which read, in its entirety, "un pamplemousse!!!"

Pamplemousse, it was true, is a pretty great word, especially as a replacement for *grapefruit*, which, when you think about it, is sort of like saying "poodledog." I wrote back that I had just made some drinks with grapefruit juice and whiskey, attaching the recipe.

"Ooh lala!!!" came the reply. "Les cocktails de pamplemousse sont tres merveilleuse!!!"

Despite the friendly preliminaries, Olivier and I were nervous. There were so many things that could go wrong, so many misunderstandings that might occur, so many misalignments that could set into permanent grievance. My people didn't really do multiple-family vacations, or for that matter family vacations, or for that matter vacations. Set in their private routines, my parents rarely so much as invited anyone over for dinner. I worried that their individualistic tendencies would conflict with the more group-oriented approach of the French contingent, veterans of the cheerfully collectivist excursions that every French institution seems to sponsor. (Violeta, as the head of her workplace's travel club, could often be found traipsing her colleagues through the churches of Prague or the canals of Venice.) Olivier, meanwhile, envisioned his clan forcing interminable seated breakfasts on mine, conscripting them into unairconditioned car rides to obscure historic sites. We were used to toggling between the families we were born into and the one we were creating, between Europe and America, but we'd never tried to inhabit them both at one time.

"C'mon," I said, unzipping my grimy ferry shorts.

I jumped into the pool. Olivier followed. He swam over to the side, and I latched on to his back, wrapping my feet around his waist and my arms around his shoulders. The house was situated on a promontory that overlooked a bay, which was guarded by a watchtower that the Genoese had built in the sixteenth century to fend off pirates. I nuzzled into the scruff of his neck, inhaling the sunshine singe.

. . .

JACQUES AND HUGO got there first.

"Can you get *magret*?" Hugo called, putting in duck breast as his choice of pizza topping as he cannonballed into the pool.

That night it was just the four of us. The next afternoon, my parents and Matt and Melissa flew in from Paris. By some stroke of luck, the moment we'd managed to gather all of our far-flung relations happened to coincide perfectly with the one in which we were in the clear to announce that we were expecting a baby. Jacques cried when we told him.

"OHMIGOD!" my mother squealed. "I should have known because there was Diet Coke in the fridge, and you totally forgot I've been off Diet Coke since my kidney stone!"

Fabrice and Anne-Laure got in around dusk. It was a sight more beautiful to me than the lavender sunset to watch my husband, his brothers, and mine beating the hell out of each other with foam noodles. Hugo was, of course, the prime object of both their abuse and their affection.

"Do you have a girlfriend these days?" somebody said.

"Well, yes, there is a girl, but I have to—how do you say—*refléchir* about her."

"Do you like her?"

"I do!"

"Okay, so then why do you have to *refléchir*?"

"Because, do you know the *boeuf bourguignon*?" Hugo said, his eyes lighting up as though he were a waiter steering a customer toward a particularly good special. "The woman is like the *boeuf bourguignon*," he said. "You cannot go too fast. If you make one-hour, it is not a good *boeuf bourguignon*. But if you make twenty-four-hour, okay, voilà."

Later, I heard my mother telling Hugo that he was going to be a "huge ladies' man."

"I'm sorry, what is a ladies' man?"

"They're going to go bananas over you, go berserk," she said, overlooking the fact that her paraphrase would probably have been incomprehensible to anyone under twenty-five, regardless of his native language.

That night we stayed on the deck, swimming and eating and drinking until late. Fabrice was explaining to the American contingent that Corsica was famous for its boars.

"You want to hear something about boars?" Melissa said.

"Always."

"My uncle owns a piece of land in North Carolina, and in the middle of this midlife crisis, he decided he had to kill a boar with his own hands. So he makes this spear, and he throws it at the boar. Well, when you throw a spear at a boar, the boar just gets mad."

"What happened?"

"Fortunately, my other uncle, who had gone with him, had brought a gun."

"Blam," my father chimed in.

"We threw it in the Brunswick stew at Thanksgiving."

"What is Brunswick stew?"

"It's, like, this soup, with a bunch of meat and vegetables in it."

"Melissa's grandmother makes it in a garbage can and serves it with a canoe paddle," Matt said.

My brother had gone in the opposite direction from me, marrying someone whose roots in the place we'd grown up ran very deep. Melissa's family had been in North Carolina for hundreds of years on both sides. Her maternal grandparents, her parents, and her aunts and uncles all lived in the same neighborhood. They had a monthly book club, whose members consisted exclusively of blood relations. After meeting me, Melissa's grandmother had taken a subscription to the *New Yorker.*

"How do you like it?" Melissa's mother asked her.

"Well, there's an awful lot about New York."

The cadences that my father had picked up over the years were Melissa's patrimony; a pack of French in-laws were, to her, an even greater inconceivability than they had been to us. Where my identity seemed subtractive (I was the remainder of a chain of migrations), hers was cumulative (the principal and the interest of people who had stayed for a long time in the same place). Matt, when he'd met her, seemed to consolidate himself. I, too, felt her ballast.

Jacques and my mother were huddled over a citronella candle, Jacques saying something about when a man loves a woman. The exchanges going on around me were dispatches from the far poles of my identity. It was as though one of the house's amenities were a satellite dish that allowed me to surf among all the channels of my existence.

"We knew, the first time we met Olivier, that he came from a *very* special family," my mother said.

I could tell that her compliment wasn't getting through.

"Mom, 'special' means more like 'weird' in French."

She looked at Jacques pleadingly.

"I meant 'special' in English!"

The candles were burning down, and the pool was getting cold. The bedtime routine was one of the junctures Olivier and I had been dreading. In his family, you weren't slinking off to your room without having *fait la bise.* In mine, you weren't kissing anybody you weren't sharing a bed with. We watched with trepidation as everyone began to take their leave.

"Good night, John," Jacques said to my father, sticking out a firm hand.

"Good night, Jacques," my father replied, planting a dainty kiss on Jacques's cheek, as eager to mirror the mores of his environment as a tennis fan dressed in whites.

He turned to Anne-Laure, who was hanging out some towels over the back of a chair.

"Want to try with me?"

FIFTY LIVRES and a hope chest containing a thousand pins, a hundred sewing needles, four lace braids, two knives, scissors, stockings, gloves, shoe ribbons, a bonnet, a headdress, a taffeta handkerchief, a comb, and a spool of white thread—this was the dowry by which Louis XIV enticed some 770 Frenchwomen to undertake passage to Quebec between 1663 and 1673. The women sailed from Dieppe and La Rochelle. Virgins and widows, they ranged in age from fourteen to fifty-nine. These *filles du roi*—daughters of the king—had a sole purpose: to marry settlers. As Jean Talon, the first intendant of New France, wrote to Jean-Baptiste Colbert, Louis's minister of finance, "It is important in the establishment of a country to sow good seed."

French brides for French subjects: the program cost the crown dearly, but the impulse was understandable. A nation does not go to the trouble of colonizing another only to let its protocols dissipate. No king aspires to be the one who lets his civilization die in a foreign land, just as no parent dreams that his child will grow up to marry someone who doesn't speak their language. The men of New France could have found wives among the native people of Canada. The colonizers were not so much concerned with genetic impurity as they were with cultural attenuation. When, after nearly a century in

North America, it became clear that Frenchmen were becoming more like the native people than the native people were becoming like Frenchmen—"We haven't obliged the savages to learn our language, rather in order to do business with them we're required to learn theirs," Colbert complained—the government brought in the *filles du roi*, girls-next-door imported across an ocean.

In 1671 alone, they bore nearly seven hundred children. Two-thirds of French Canadians are descended from one or more of them. Ambroisine Doigt. Marguerite Bonnefoy. Etoinette Lamoureaux. Marie-Rose Vivien, Marie-Rogère Lepage, Marie-Perette Lauriot, Marie-Anne Poussin. There was even a Brazilian-born woman, baptized in Portugal, named Espérance Du Rosaire—unable to sign her name, referred to as "the moor." They must have been so lonely. More than half of them had lost their fathers. Many of them came from Paris's Salpêtrière charity hospital, whose poorer wards slept three to five to a bed. Marie de l'Incarnation, who led the Ursuline sisters of Quebec, wrote that the city girls, especially, struggled to adjust: "We no longer wish to ask for any girls except those from villages, suited for men's work. Experience has led us to see those who were not raised up for it, who were not suited for [life] here, being in a misery out from which they cannot pull themselves." The shift from an urban environment to a rural one, though, was surely the least of their disorientations.

But getting on a ship, crouching in the hold with the livestock during squalls, risking dysentery and scurvy, to arrive in a frigid wilderness where food was so scarce that one might die of scurvy anyway represented to them an opportunity. The women were virtually guaranteed marriages and families that they likely would not have otherwise made. Theirs was a conservative maneuver, a great risk taken in the service of perpetuating the past rather than breaking from it. The first question a *fille du roi* asked of a suitor was, "Have you built a home upon your land?" Remote as it was, New France was a chance at continuity. Their patrimonies might be preserved.

VIOLETA AND TEDDY ARRIVED—she in a white lace dress, he in a pressed guayabera. They got changed and joined everyone on the patio. Teddy was wearing a budgie smuggler, but my family played it cool. Violeta had gone for a conservative look in a fringed tangerine bikini. It was a mellow morning—my father dozing, a book on his chest; Matt and Fabrice beached side by side on a pair of loungers, overworked young professionals catching up on rest. We were all sun worshipers, with the exception of my mother. She was sitting in the shade with her iPad.

"I'm sending pictures of Corsica to all my friends!" she said. "Oh, look, an e-mail from Marie."

Marie was a neighbor my mother often ran into on her morning walks, chanting along to the French tapes.

"Are you throwing tomatoes yet?" she read aloud. "Also are you having lots of fun? I hope you all are having a wonderful time. Hi to John, Matt, Lauren & O, and Melissa."

I recognized the "O" dodge—the sign of a correspondent who couldn't quite figure out Olivier's name. It was an understandable move. A friend had once written to me ahead of a journey to Wilmington, wishing "a safe trip to you and Olivia."

"What's she talking about, 'tomatoes'?"

"Not sure!" my mom replied. "I'll write back and ask."

The next e-mail from Marie had the subject line "Wrong country."

"Just realized Corsica is in Italy," she wrote. "Thinking it was Spain where it is tomato day. Pictured all of you in red from tossing tomatoes at each other."

ACTUALLY, some parents do dream of their children growing up to marry someone who speaks a different language. The Tukanoan people of the Northwest Amazon divide themselves into sixteen different patrilineal descent groups, each of which speaks one of sixteen languages. According to Tukanoan mythology, the sixteen groups arose at the beginning of time, when the "first people" came from the east in an anaconda-shaped canoe. Having conquered the waters of the underworld, they ascended the Vaupés River. At each stop along the way, the ancestors of a specific language group got out of the canoe and began to settle the area. This etiology jibes with the historical likelihood that, fleeing the Portuguese in the eighteenth century, various Tukanoan tribes sought refuge in the upper Vaupés. Living in proximity, and with common enemies, they consider themselves a single people. They maintain separate roles within the culture, however, by practicing linguistic exogamy—the requirement that a man marry a woman from a different language group.

All Tukanoans are multilingual, speaking at least three languages, including Tukano, the regional lingua franca. When a woman marries, she moves to her husband's longhouse and takes on his language. A child's parents never come from the same language group. There is a strong taboo against mixing languages—a woman who lets Barà words creep into a Tuyuka conversation, for example, will be chided for setting a bad example for her offspring. As the anthropologist Jean E. Jackson explains in *The Fish People*, her study of life in a

Tukanoan longhouse from 1969 to 1972, "Although everyone is multilingual, individuals identify with and are loyal to only one language, their father language." When Jackson asked a Tukanoan why his people continued to speak so many languages, when they could all speak Tukano, he replied, "If we all were Tukano speakers, where would we get our women?" As obvious as the arrangement is to the Tukanoan, it leaves the non-Tukanoan mystified. Why, with hammocks to weave and manioc to mash, do they persist in maintaining sixteen languages when one would suffice? Why is the marriage of two speakers of the same language an impossibility, as incestuous as the union of a brother and a sister would be to us?

The organization of Tukanoan society suggests that language is not culture. But at the same time it enacts a sort of intuitive linguistic relativism, a conviction that languages are fundamental delimiters of people, and that some advantage lies in the preservation of their differences.

Jackson describes night in a Tukanoan longhouse as a "well-orchestrated choral piece, featuring dog barks, baby cries, coughs, farts, laughter, bad dreams, conversation, goings and comings (which involve lifting the heavy door each time), replenishing the fire, and songs." Attending a festival, she recalls, "Our longhouse group had been crowded into a single small house with two other groups of visitors, and during the evening one woman suddenly became seriously ill. She started screaming with pain (the aspirin I gave her had no visible effect) and continued to scream all night. Throughout, her companions played two different radios at full volume, and all of the men stayed up processing coca, smoking, drinking manioc beer, and laughing." Jackson writes that although these juxtapositions made her uncomfortable, they were probably for the best. The woman didn't feel pressure to manage her screams, on top of her pain, and the men didn't have to stifle their revelry, creating resentment. The cacophony was actually something harmonious. Perhaps Babel finally gets built in a riot.

VIOLETA AND TEDDY had been to Corsica several times. Wanting to make sure that my parents didn't miss out on the sights, they volunteered to take them to Bonifacio, a citadel town about an hour down the coast. Nobody else felt like going. Olivier and I would have joined them, but we'd promised to accompany the rest of the group to the beach. We were skeptical of the idea of the four of them setting off alone, with no obvious way to communicate. Besides, they would have to take our car. My parents had never driven in a non-English-speaking country; Violeta and Teddy had never driven an automatic transmission. Olivier gave Teddy a brief tutorial, and off they went, lurching down the driveway.

At the beach, we rented paddleboards, gondoliering ourselves around for hours in the midday glare. We could hear helicopters, buzzing off to attend to a brush fire. The afternoon lazed into evening, the sun still high, as we drank cold Pietras at a snack bar shaded by Corsican pines.

"*Putain*, it's six thirty!" Olivier said, herding everyone into the car.

We sped back to the house.

"Coucou?" Olivier called out, jiggling the key in the lock.

Nobody was there.

As we envisioned disaster scenarios, our parents were driving up the N198. The men were in the front, speaking fragmented Spanish, my father's originating from high school and Teddy's from classes at the Andernos community center. The women were in the back, chatting away in some sort of international mom language. They had been talking for six hours.

"Bonifacio was *amazing*," my mother said, stumbling in the door.

"That's great, Sue," Olivier said, relaxing for the first time all day. "What did you do?"

She fished her phone out of her bag and started swiping through the photo gallery.

"We went to lunch in this little restaurant, and then we went to a church, and then we did this long walk on this staircase that's cut into the cliffs. Oh, there were these weird piles of rocks! I couldn't figure out what they were—like somebody was building a kiln?"

"What's a kiln?" Olivier said.

At last: kryptonite. I'd heard Olivier make little mistakes before—they often had the effect of improving upon the term in question, as in "mind melt," or "This place is a Dumpster," or thinking that the abbreviation for our accountant Arthur's name was Arth—but I'd never seen him genuinely stumped. *Kiln*—a four-letter noun meaning that our vulnerability was mutual; that the burden of learning, forever regenerating like laundry, was shared; that from now on I was going to start talking about pottery whenever I felt myself on the losing end of a linguistic power struggle. Kiln!

That night we cooked out on the patio. Hugo, having somehow turned the pool lights to a disco setting, was practicing his jackknifes. Fabrice and Anne-Laure were giving Matt and Melissa tips on Paris restaurants while my father manned the grill. Olivier, ever vigilant, circulated like a maître d'. I was sitting with my mother and Violeta, who were discussing the care of the elderly in different parts of the world.

"Il y a quinze ans je suis allée en Chine et les maisons de retraite m'ont beaucoup impressionnées," Violeta was saying.

"So, Violeta went to China fifteen years ago, and the nursing homes there were really nice," I said.

"Really?" my mother said. "I'm so surprised."

"Ah bon?" I repeated. "Ça m'etonne."

Olivier had sneaked up behind me.

"Lauren can translate!" he said, seeming as proud as he was shocked.

"Je peux traduire!"

"That's—"

Over by the grill, a dance party had broken out. Rihanna was blasting from the stereo. Melissa, Hugo, and Matt, shouting out the lyrics, had formed a kickline. Fabrice was raising the roof with a pair of tongs. My father and Anne-Laure had found a broomstick, which they were using as a maypole.

CORSICA IS IN FRANCE. It has been since 1769, when the French army defeated Corsican irregulars, led by Pascal Paoli, at the Battle of Ponte Novu. Carlo Buonaparte, an attorney, and his wife, Letizia, had been on the bridge—the Corsicans, according to Voltaire, reloaded their muskets behind a barricade built of corpses—fighting to preserve the independent republic that Paoli had declared fourteen years earlier. The battle lost, they joined a fleeing cortège. Carlo carried a gourd of water and a dagger. Letizia had a baby boy, Joseph, lying in a saddle basket and was six months pregnant. They endured weeks of snow and rain, hard bread in cold caves. As they forded a swollen river, Letizia's mule lost its footing, and she and her children were almost swept away. This was May. By late summer the party had made it to Ajaccio, where on August 15 Letizia went into labor during mass. Napoleon, who would later Frenchify the family name, was born almost immediately, with a large head and weak legs.

Pascal Paoli, in exile in London, was greeted as a hero. "I was, for the rest of my life, set free from a slavish timidity in the presence of great men, for where shall I find a man greater than Paoli?" Boswell wrote in *An Account of Corsica*, a blockbuster of the time. (During Boswell's lifetime, the book outsold his biography of Dr. Johnson.) In America, one of the founding members of the Sons of Liberty named his son Paschal Paoli McIntosh. Revolutionaries met at General Paoli's Tavern, in Paoli, Pennsylvania, where "Remember Paoli" was spelled out in copper pennies hammered into the floor.

Corsica is "a mountain in a sea"—easy to invade, impossible to subdue. Its earliest inhabitants left dolmens and menhirs, somber monuments that seem to warn one off the island like scarecrows. In 540 BC, the Greeks arrived. The Romans succeeded them in 237. Over nearly a millennium, Corsica absorbed and repelled the conquests of the Vandals, the Ostrogoths, the Lombards, the Aragonians, and the Saracens. In 1284 the Genoans wrested the island from the Pisans, ruling, with fluctuating degrees of control, until Paoli's declaration of sovereignty in 1755, after which they handed it to France in a secret deal. Corsica has always been an anomaly: a birthplace of constitutional democracy and the last bastion of the vendetta, where seafaring cosmopolitanism coexists with *montagnard* distrust. It is a site of strange amalgamations: the priest reciting the sacraments with pistols on the altar, the eel that is said to mate with the snake, the fisherman who can't swim. Admiral Nelson lost an eye there.

The island's motley culture has long sat uneasily within the centralized one of mainland France. After the world wars a nationalist movement arose that has lobbied for the past half century, often violently, for Corsican independence. In 1998 the *préfet* of Corsica was assassinated—three bullets in the neck—on his way home from the theater. His killer was not apprehended until 2003, when images from an infrared camera led police to the mountains, where he had been hiding in a shepherd's hut.

The centerpiece of the Corsican nationalist movement is the preservation and revival of the Corsican language. Like French, it derives from Latin, but it is heavily influenced by Italian dialects, mainly Tuscan. Italian speakers can follow Corsican, but French speakers can't. Corsicans speak French, but many of them consider it a colonial imposition, as one nationalist wrote, "a pretentious language that has nourished itself on the cadavers of other languages." Though only 65 percent of them speak Corsican, it remains the repository of their heritage and the emblem of their pride. Another Corsican graffito reads "Morta a lingua, mortu u populu"—Kill a language, kill a people. On the island's bilingual road signs, it is common to see French place-names painted over in black.

Corsica is sparsely populated, but somehow it's a loud place, the host of a racket as layered and heterogeneous as the maquis's scent. In all the noise, articulation is crucial: lore has it that the *mazzeri*—local seers who could both predict death and inflict it—were the products of botched baptisms, at which the priest had bungled the words or the godparents repeated them imprecisely. Until the late nineteenth century, Corsican was primarily a spoken language. One of its most cherished expressions is the ancient tradition of polyphonic singing, in which, under the right conditions, the voices of four singers combine to conjure an invisible interlocutor—the "ghost tone" or "fifth voice."

"LET'S BREAK THIS UP," Olivier said, padding out onto the patio to the sight of a table laid with napkins and forks.

We were a two-person *decryptage* unit, experts at extracting meaning from the slightest clues.

"What does *éclabousser* mean?" I'd ask.

"Like when you jump on a pond," Olivier would say.

"Oh, 'splashing'!" I'd respond, rapid-fire. There was no one in the world who could have bested us in a game of Taboo.

Violeta and Teddy were waiting for breakfast to begin. Olivier approached them, explaining quietly that Americans, at least the ones with whom they were vacationing, typically began their days by walking into the kitchen and eating such things as granola bars and leftover egg rolls. The French chef Jacques Pépin, spending the weekend at Craig Claiborne's house in the 1960s, had greeted this sort of program—the poached eggs kept in a bowl of ice water; the sandwich fixings; the pouring oneself a glass of wine in the afternoon—as a liberation from the "ordeal" of the rigidly structured French meal. Olivier's family seemed less sure. Still, they proceeded to the kitchen. Posted against the countertops, the table gone but their orientation to it and each other replicated precisely, they appeared to be throwing an underwater tea party in the air.

The Americans, unbriefed by me, gravitated toward the patio. The seated breakfast, drawing converts, had prevailed. Every morning Teddy and my father, in silence or Spanish, made a joint mission to the *boulangerie*. Croissants were eaten. Baguettes were broken. Exotic beverages, hot and cold, were drunk.

"I had some of that sparkling water," my mother told me. "It was actually pretty good."

One morning, as we picked at the remains of a watermelon, the conversation turned toward the baby, who would be the first grandchild, the first niece or nephew, on either side. My brother, it emerged, was not a fan of women breastfeeding in public.

"You're not going to do that, are you?" he said.

"Matt, you're not wearing a shirt right now," I replied.

Melissa jumped in.

"What is it about seeing a woman's breast in public that bothers you?"

"I don't know, it's awkward."

"Breastfeeding—it's a question of having the desire to do it," Violeta added, speaking in French, with Olivier translating. "It's a moment of complicity between the mother and the child, a moment of pleasure that's not with a lover. There's nothing like it."

"I think your breasts will triple in size," Hugo chimed in.

"Matt, are you possessive?" Violeta went on. "It's not erotic in the least."

"She's throwing oil on the fire," Olivier whispered into my ear. He refused to continue translating.

We could have listened to the argument all morning, though—the categories that had defined our life together dissolving and realigning, languages melding, allegiances shifting from French and English into women and men. The addends of our backgrounds didn't cancel out into neutrality.

French plus American was not Swiss. Violeta got out her iPhone and started playing a Georges Brassens song about a woman nursing a cat.

I HAD SEEN A SIGN nailed to a telephone pole, advertising a traditional Corsican concert in Solenzara, a village about forty minutes from the house. It was to start at nine thirty, a tough time to tear a crowd away from poolside cocktails, but I was determined to go. I started lobbying the household. One by one, people acquiesced. The night of the show, the dozen of us crammed into two cars and set off for Solenzara.

We arrived at Saint-Paul, a modest church just uphill from the village port, a neon blur of ice cream parlors and promenading families. We paid admission and entered through a wooden door into what had once been a stable, where the village monks had allowed travelers to board the horses that transported hauled logs downriver from the mountains to the coast. An iron cross, like a weathervane, topped a stone bell tower. The sanctuary was tiny—a nave, with a checkerboard floor, that ran directly into the altar, a simple table cov ered with a linen cloth. Oak beams girded the ceiling. Painted wooden statues of the apostles adorned whitewashed walls.

We hustled into the pews just as the leader of the group was introducing the first song. Its title, he said, was "Cantu eternu"—the island's eternal song, linked to the land, to a way of life, to the calls of the shepherds, ricocheting from one valley to the next. The group consisted of four men, dressed in black jeans and black button-down shirts. They could have been bouncers. They moved close together, forming a half-moon. Then the shortest among them cupped a hand to his ear, as though he were listening to a seashell, and gave the pitch.

"*Issu cantu di a terra*," he began in a clear bass. "*Hè muscu di a vita*," he sang, drawing the syllables out several notes, adding almost Arabic-sounding melismas, as strong and delicate as the scrollwork on an iron gate.

A second voice came in, higher and quavering.

"*S'hè pisato la mio voce*," he sang, as the other three rocked him on a hammock of sound. The music was so full, so filling, that I felt the roof might lift off the church.

There were laments and lullabies. One song memorialized Maria Ghjentile—the Corsican Antigone, a teenager who in 1769 risked her life by giving a proper burial to her fiancé, a resistance fighter who had been tortured by the French and left in the street to die.

The singers moved into the middle of the church. The lead singer struck a low note, and some of the members of the audience stood up, clasping their hands and joining in. Having not really understood the introduction, I assumed it was another eulogy. Olivier explained later that it had been the Corsican national anthem.

After the concert, we walked across the street to a pizzeria and ordered pies to take back to the house. They were slow in coming, and while we waited, we loitered on the restaurant's terrace. A band was playing rock music. My dad was teaching Hugo movie lines.

"I coulda been a contenda," he said.

"I cood 'ave bean ze contender," Hugo echoed back.

"I coulda been a contenda!"

"I cood 'ave bean ze contender!"

We got the pizzas and piled back into the cars. The radio crackled. Hot wind whooshed through the windows. Conversations, bleeding into each other, rose and fell. I heard bombs and bumblebees, polemics and punch lines, the buzzing of a thousand organisms far and near. Amid the din, I thought I could just make out an extra voice—our own complex polyphony, which sounded like none of us and all of us, the cry of something not from the hereafter but right on the cusp of life.

Seven

THE FUTURE

Le Futur

"ALLEZ, ALLEZ," a woman will be screaming into your ear. You will feel like it's the Albertville Games of 1992, and you're in the luge competition. All that will be missing is the cowbell.

"La première fois, bien, mais la deuxième, zéro!" the woman will say as you push, joining her thumb and pointer finger together to make the international sign for zilch.

It will be the end of March. Someone will have given you zwieback for breakfast. You will be in a white room with casement windows. Beyond a scrim of branches—some scratchily aloof type of yew you never saw as a child—you will glimpse the late-afternoon sun demulsifying, a mansard roof. For a minute you will wonder where you are. Then you will hear the doctor call for *la ventouse.* The word refers to a thing you never will have heard of, in any language, until a few weeks earlier. You will later identify it, in English, as the vacuum extractor that facilitates a vacuum-assisted delivery (of a baby, not a *cafetière*).

Your thinking will start to muddle like that. Your speech

will become an admixture, your private thesaurus a dual-language edition, like one of those airline magazines with two contiguous columns of type.

"ALLEZ, ALLEZ, ALLEZ!" Olivier will yell, strong and low and urgent. "AL-LEEEEEEEEEZ!"

You will push with everything you've got: *la ventouse* must be averted, zilch lady must be shown what's up. Twenty seconds later, the blood, the cry, the perfect head. The doctor will take her. She will be cleaned and dressed.

"Mon amour!" Olivier will cry, rifling through the bag you've packed. "Did you forget to bring her underwear?"

"Babies don't wear underwear," you will reply, too dazed to try to figure out what word he's searching for, what he really means to ask.

"Ah, okay!"

You will realize he actually meant underwear, not diaper, that gender can be a sinkhole to the language gap.

The doctor will give her back to you, smelling of petals. You will hold her to your chest as though she could stop your heart from falling out. You will have given birth in French.

IF SOMEONE had told me this story, twenty or ten or even two years ago, I never would have accepted myself as its protagonist. How could the woman laboring to the sounds of a third-group verb be me, how could *ma fille*—in French, my daughter and my girl—be destined to fill in forms for the rest of her days with the birthplace Chêne-Bougeries? You imagine the events of your life against certain backdrops: the kiss on the bus, the graduation in the auditorium, the wedding at the church. Most people's projections turn out to be somewhere in the ballpark.

When they're not, the effect can be as disorienting as time travel: America in the Pleistocene era would have seemed only slightly less likely a setting for the birth of my first child than a clinic in a Swiss suburb.

Jacques drove all night to see us. He arrived, stubble-cheeked and elated, spent an hour, and turned right back around to make it back to work. Violeta gave me a diamond necklace. She had had it made from her late mother's engagement ring. When she and Teddy left, they stashed a pot-au-feu in our refrigerator.

"Would you like to place an announcement in the newspaper?" a hospital administrator asked.

We declined, not knowing anyone who took *Le Chênois*. But the question moved me, presuming, as it did, that our daughter's existence would be of interest to people other than us, that she was already part of something, even if we weren't.

We should have said yes. It was a kind gesture. Besides, I was a fiend for birth announcements, wedding announcements, and obituaries, the "hatch, match, and dispatch" trinity that once comprised the only three times a respectable woman's name should appear in print. I read them with the attention that other people devote to important novels. It fascinated me to think about the way the lives of others hewed to or swerved from their probable trajectories, how they were or were not products of the shaping forces of time, family, and place. The greatest one I ever came across paid tribute to Giorgio Carbone, "a bewhiskered grower of mimosa from a family of mimosa growers," who had proclaimed Seborga, a five-square-mile patch of northwest Italy, an independent principality, and convinced his neighbors to elect him prince for life, calling him His Tremendousness.

Our insurance policy provided for five days at the clinic, a standard stay in Switzerland. The morning after the *accouchement*, I heard a knock at the door.

"Entrez."

"Quel menu préféreriez-vous?" a woman in white scrubs asked, handing me a printed sheet. "Première suggestion ou deuxième?"

I scanned the offerings—two choices for each meal. For lunch did I want *carpaccio de boeuf à l'huile de truffe, saumon d'Ecosse sauce coriandre, blé aux herbes, blettes à la tomate, et tarte fine aux pommes* (beef carpaccio with truffle oil, Scottish salmon with cilantro sauce, buckwheat with herbs, chard with tomatoes, and an apple tart), or *salade frisée et madeleine au parmesan, suprême de volaille au gingembre, pommes purée, carottes jaunes, et mousse fromage blanc et coulis de framboises* (endive salad with a parmesan cracker, ginger chicken, mashed potatoes, yellow carrots, and cream cheese mousse with raspberry sauce)?

"Hmm," I said, trying to keep a straight face. "La première, si vous plaît."

Half an hour later, a second knock, *très discret*. Another woman in white, hovering in the doorway.

"Bonjour, Madame. Je suis l'esthéticienne."

"Pardon?"

"L'esthéticienne."

"Oh," I said, comprehending now that she was some kind of beautician.

"Je n'ai pas pris de rendezvous," I told her. "Vous vous êtes trompée de chambre."

She did indeed have the right room, she explained, and I did have an appointment—each new mother was entitled to a *soin postnatal*, just a little pick-me-up to help her feel more like herself. Would I like a manicure, a pedicure, a foot massage, or to have my hair done?

I chose the foot massage, feeling like the years in Switzerland might actually have been worth it.

When our daughter was old enough to travel, we took her to Andernos for a weekend. Violeta and Teddy thought that she was "superbe." They had set up a changing table, a crib, a mobile—the works. When I walked into the bathroom, I realized that they had been on a full-fledged home-improvement kick. I am quite sure that it was their desire to experiment with new technologies, in the seventh and eighth decades of their lives, rather than their fumbling daughter-in-law, that had led them to put in a stand-up shower.

Olivier and I, with Hugo, took Jacques out for a birthday dinner. The restaurant was across the bay from Violeta and Teddy's village. To get there we called a water taxi, which sped us through the twilight, eyes watering and hair tangling, just as *les pinasses*—the brightly colored, snub-nosed wooden boats of the region—began to deliquesce, blue and then black, into the horizon. After forty minutes we reached the opposite side of the peninsula. Ten feet from land, the driver cut his motor.

"Allez-y!" he ordered.

We jumped into the water, shoes in our hands, splashing into the foamy shallows where the sea lapped the shore. Behind us loomed the Dune du Pilat, a three-hundred-foot massif of sand. We walked down the beach. When we reached the end, we ascended through pine forest to a lookout point. There, the restaurant twinkled in the distance. To enter it, we passed through a courtyard equipped with a giant chessboard, pawns and queens and rooks the size of fire hydrants. The place had a dreamlike quality, a purity of mood. Tea lights flickered under billowing canopies. Everything was white.

It was an enchanted night, even by the standards of people who had not been on house arrest for a quarter of a year. After oysters and Champagne, meat and wine, cake and coffee, we made our way back to the water to catch our ride. It was long past midnight. Earlier, the beach had been deserted, but now it teemed with people, a nocturnal society of campers and surf fishermen, their illuminated lures arcing like comets as they cast. Olivier and I stopped and stared up at the moon, orange and gibbous. Phantasmagorical clouds passed over it: a shark fin, the exposed root of a tooth.

"I'm ready," I said, my voice catching.

It had been a while since I'd been on a beach at night, or had more than half a glass of wine.

"I just want to figure out where we're going to be and find a place and never move."

I stopped, aware that weepiness, as a mode of expression, never went over well with Olivier. But he pulled me close.

"I do, too."

THAT SUMMER, we went to North Carolina. I'd left America a heartsick monoglot. I was returning with a husband and a daughter and a second language that, for the rest of the members of my new family, was a native tongue. In the five years that I'd been living abroad, I hadn't been home for more than a week. We planned to stay a month.

I flew with our daughter, backtracking the journey it had taken me years to make: Geneva to London to Raleigh-Durham, a two-hour drive from my parents' place. (Olivier was joining us later.) The trip took fifteen hours. On the plane I screamed, having become convinced that her foot was caught, perhaps fatally, in the airplane seat's armrest; she didn't. At last I stumbled through the doors of the baggage claim, bearing three suitcases, two carry-ons, a diaper bag, a stroller, and a surprisingly unfazed four-month-old.

"How was it?" my mother asked, once we'd completed a reunion so gaspingly tearful as to resemble, in the age of Skype, a historical reenactment of the airport pickups of the 1980s.

Pas mal, I thought.

"Not bad," I said.

I was so glad to be there. Having a child had provoked in me, as it does in many people, a renewed connection to my own childhood, a longing for its trappings and comforts. I had spent hours and dumb amounts of money importing baby products from America, not because I thought American baby products were necessarily better, but because I wanted everything to be just the way it was. I was craving familiarity and—had been, going on a year—fried chicken and biscuits. Toward the end of my pregnancy, I'd had the car keys in hand, prepared to make the not-insubstantial drive to the closest Kentucky Fried Chicken, in Chambéry, France. (Switzerland, among its other privations, did not have a KFC franchise.) Fortunately I Googled the menu before I left. In France, the traditional accompaniment to fried chicken is French fries, corn, or a salad.

These were just the most recent manifestations of a persistent malady, a generalized homesickness that craved not so much any particular home as it did a home, period. As thrilled as I was to be in America, I had been gone too far and too long to slot effortlessly back into life there. There was always something that gave me pause, that made me feel like a geographical Rip Van Winkle. This time it was online shopping—not its existence, but its variety and ease. Free shipping and overnight delivery on an SPF 2500 beach umbrella? Yes, please.

My enthusiasm for buying things on the Internet was such that the credit card company put a block on my account. One afternoon I called to ask them to lift it.

"Sorry," I said when my daughter's crying became audible in the background. "I've got a new baby."

"I could not be happier for you and your family!" the operator replied. "Is this gonna be your first or your last?"

Eventually, he agreed to rescind the block.

"It has truly been a pleasure and a privilege serving you, and I hope that I've done nothing but offer you amazing customer service," he said. "Have yourself an awesome day, much love to you and your family, and thanks for doing business with American Express."

The operator was being friendly, but I was flabbergasted. To my French-tuned ear, his familiarity sounded crazily presumptuous—the ultimate *tutoyer*. I tried to figure out who was the weirdo: him or me. Was he an outlier, or was this the way my countrypeople now spoke? Or had they always spoken like this, and I was only beginning to notice?

At breakfast the next morning I grabbed the local section of the *Morning Star*. "New Castle Hayne Intersection a Circle of Confusion," the headline of the lead story declared. A roundabout had been constructed in Castle Hayne, a nearby community. Local drivers were having trouble figuring it out. The article gave an eyewitness report on the confusion and then turned to a question-and-answer format:

"What are roundabouts?"

"What do drivers in Castle Hayne think?"

"How do I drive in one?"

"Are there others around here?"

WE WENT TO THE BEACH almost every afternoon, always at the same spot, in front of a club we belonged to. It was a delight to take up my old summer routine, playing Ping-Pong and eating Oreo ice cream sandwiches. En route to the snack bar one afternoon, I saw a thirtysomething woman chasing an adorable little girl in a smocked dress and Velcro sneakers. She was one of a set of identical twins who were a couple of years older than I and—along with their first cousins, a set of identical twin boys—had pretty much run the place in our youth.

The little girl was eating some chocolate. The mother scolded her, not harshly.

Turning to me in mock frustration, she moaned, "Can you believe she ganked my Reesie's Cups?"

It's *Reese's* Cups, I wanted to say, the fourteen-year-old pedant in me reawakening. Hearing "ganked" was as stirringly embarrassing as hearing a song you used to like come on the radio without warning. In the argot of our adolescence, the word had meant taken, swiped, stolen, snagged. I was at once jangled by and a little envious of the blitheness with which my old acquaintance deployed it. The audacity of using a bit of slang that had enjoyed a minute of fame twenty years earlier, and assuming that everyone would understand! But she had earned it. This was the prerogative of those who stayed: to never have to consider their audience.

It wasn't just other people's speech that struck me. Olivier and I had always been careful to avoid mixing our languages—a phrase we'd once come across, *triste sabir* (sad pidgin), haunted us both. But there, in my parents' kitchen, in Toys "R" Us, in the living rooms of my oldest friends, the French words came spilling out. *Sucette*: I reached for it before "pacifier." *Téter*, a verb purpose-built for recounting the habits of a nursing infant, whereas in English I never knew whether I was supposed to say she had "eaten" or "drunk." I had acquired an entire maternal lexicon, the legacy of those early days in the clinic, that came to me first in French. The word *nourrisson* touched some tender spot in me. Its little-used English equivalent, *suckling*, emphasized the draining qualities of a newborn, made one seem like a job, but when I heard *nourrisson*, I focused on what I could give rather than what she was taking, remembered that to care for her was my privilege. Willing myself out of bed in the dark, small hours, I thought, *Ma petite nourrisson.*

People didn't quite know what to make of us. We might have been human roundabouts. Melissa, my sister-in-law, told me that she had been down at the courthouse, filing some motions.

"Are you going to the bar association meeting?" one of the clerks of court had asked.

"I can't," Melissa said. "My sister-in-law's in town."

"Oh," the clerk replied. "Is she the one that married a prince?"

Once I would have been mortified, but now I found the story amusing. I was proud of the alliances I'd forged, the mongrel family we were making, the happy gobbledygook that we spoke. Wilmington had even gotten a wine bar. One of the appetizers on offer was a plate of tuna, mixed greens, potatoes, egg, and green beans: "Salad Niçoise (nee-suaz)," the menu read.

. . .

PER THE COMMAND OF THE Consulat Général de France à Genève, I presented myself at room 18 of the Lycée Rodolphe Töpffer at precisely two o'clock to undergo an assessment of my acquaintance with *la langue française et des valeurs de la République*. I had spent the past twenty-four hours cramming, mostly on websites for Moroccan brides, even though the woman at the consulate had told us that she doubted I'd have any problem.

"The questions are, for example, 'Can a woman divorce her husband in France?' "

"Yes!" I'd replied.

"No!" Olivier had shouted.

He thought it was hilarious that I had to prove my mastery of the values of his civilization, kept teasing me while I was studying.

"Name three acceptable breakfast foods," he'd say.

"How much perfume must one put on before leaving the house?"

"In France, is a woman allowed to wear yoga pants when she is not doing yoga?"

I was more nervous than I had been in years. At the Lycée Rodolphe Töpffer, I swallowed a tickly laugh. The soles of my feet broke into a sweat. This was it, the ultimate French test, the stuff anxiety dreams were made of. The fact that the school was styled as a Swiss chalet, with potted geraniums and lace curtains, didn't help. What if I never got out of this place? What if I turned on the French faucet and nothing came out? I almost threw up in a birdbath.

We took our seats at wooden desks. Next to mine hung a child's poster illustrating the Battle of Verdun. The examiner, a well-put-together woman with frosted hair and bows on her shoes, handed out worksheets. I understood when she said that we had ten minutes to complete them. The first part of the test was simple enough. I gave my name, my date of birth, my place of birth; I filled in the blanks of a dialogue set in a consulate; I reshuffled *demande*, *son*, *de*, *renouvellement*, *le*, *il*, and *passeport* to read "Il demande le renouvellement de son passport." Composing a noun-heavy thirty words about what I put in my suitcase when I travel, I even managed a little furbelow about not forgetting to pack a book.

We handed in our papers and left the room, waiting to be called back, one by one, for the oral evaluation. This was the gut-roiling portion, the road test to the theory quiz. I knew that I could speak coherent if not faultless French, but I didn't know whether I could do it under conscious observation. I sat on a bench, surrounded by concrete cherubim, thinking about all the decisions I'd made that had led me to this particular faux-alpine garden on a sunny Saturday afternoon. The test felt less like a scholastic drill than a referendum on my life choices.

The woman who went before me had offered, by way of small talk, that she was a professional interpreter. I watched her through the classroom window, confidently nodding her head.

"Madame Collins?" the examiner at last called out.

I entered the classroom.

"Bonjour, Madame," I said, in the punctiliously stilted manner of a driver being sure to honk before she backs out.

"Bonjour. Et vous venez d'où?"

I was American, I told her. My husband was French. We had a daughter. I stuck to the script, but I talked as though I were writing. Whenever I made a mistake, I tried to go back and fix it, to verbally wield a red pen.

"Nous sommes déménagés—pardon, nous avons déménagés—à Genève de Londres—il y a presque trois ans,"

I said, explaining, with more emphasis on auxiliary verbs than content, that we had been in Geneva almost three years. I pronounced *semaine* like *semen*. I swapped an *encore* for a *toujours*. But my small talk evidently sufficed. We would move on to the values section, the examiner announced.

Hit me, I thought. I could name the eight presidents of the Fifth Republic; tell you the significance of July 14, 1789. I knew that polygamy didn't fly in France.

"If someone promulgates hatred, can this be punished by the law?" the examiner began.

I wasn't really sure what she was saying. "Free speech!" the American on my shoulder said, grabbing at key words. "No, inciting racial hatred!" the French person countered.

"Sorry, could you repeat the question?"

"If someone incites racial hatred, makes a hate speech, can he be punished by the law?"

I paused for a second.

"Yes?"

The examiner, I saw, marked my response correct, and continued to the next question.

"Do men and women have the same rights?"

"Yes."

"Can a foreigner be president?"

"No."

"When you pay taxes in France, do they support museums?"

"Yes, they do."

"Name three well-known French people."

"Jean Dujardin, Gad Elmaleh . . ."

For some reason, all I could think of were celebrities, the covers of *Closer* and *Voici*, the trashy French magazines that Olivier always bought before a flight.

"Marion Cotillard!"

The examiner regarded me over lime-green bifocals.

"Americans always say Marion Cotillard."

Five days later I arrived for my appointment at the consulate. The woman behind the desk handed me a large white envelope. Inside were two certificates, issued by the minister of the interior, attesting that, per Article L.411-8 of the Code de l'Entrée, I had demonstrated sufficient familiarity with the French language and the values of the Republic. I opened my passport. The woman pasted a visa on an empty page, papering over a bald eagle. I could still see a clipper ship, racing toward the shore under a John Paul Jones quote that read, "It seems to be a law of nature, inflexible and inexorable, that those who will not risk cannot win." She indicated that I was free to go. It was official. We were moving to Paris.

Acknowledgments

MAYBE THE GREATEST PLEASURE of writing is reading. So many brilliant books informed (and, in many cases, formed) my understanding of the subjects at hand in this memoir. The following works made my thinking sharper and my memories more meaningful. I'm grateful to their authors.

In Chapter One: *Byron and the Romantics in Switzerland*, by Elma Dangerfield; *After Babel*, by George Steiner; *Passing Time*, by Michel Butor; and *Hotel du Lac*, by Anita Brookner. (Bonus reading for Switzerland skeptics: *Doctor Fischer of Geneva or The Bomb Party*, Graham Greene's novella about a toothpaste baron who throws a series of grotesque dinner parties at his lakeside villa.)

In Chapter Two: *Grammar and Good Taste*, by Dennis E. Baron; *Bilingual Public Schooling in the United States*, Paul J. Ramsey; *Language Loyalties*, edited by James Crawford; *Hold Your Tongue*, by James Crawford; *When the United States Spoke French*, by François Furstenberg; *The Tongue-Tied American*, by Paul Simon; *Letters from an American Farmer*, by J. Hector

St. John de Crèvecoeur; *The German Element in the United States*, by Albert Bernhardt Faust; *An Introduction to Cognitive Linguistics*, by Friedrich Ungerer and Hans-Jorg Schmid; *The Cambridge History of the English Language, Volume VI*, edited by John Algeo; and *The Stanford Encyclopedia of Philosophy*, a Web-based resource whose principal editor is Edward N. Zalta.

In Chapter Three: *French Ways and Their Meaning*, by Edith Wharton; *Jean Racine*, by John Sayer; *White House Interpreter*, by Harry Obst; *Found in Translation*, by Nataly Kelly and Jost Zetzsche; *The Origins of Simultaneous Interpretation*, by Francesca Gaiba; *Speak, Memory*, by Vladimir Nabokov; *The Smile Revolution*, by Colin Jones; and my trusty Larousse for help in deciphering secondhand love letters.

In Chapter Four: *Flaubert and an English Governess*, by Hermia Oliver; *Victoria & Abdul*, by Shrabani Basu; *Jigsaw*, by Sybille Bedford; *Romance Languages*, by Ti Alkire and Carol Rosen; *Empires of the Word*, by Nicholas Ostler; *Eight Months on Ghazzah Street*, by Hilary Mantel; *When the World Spoke French*, by Marc Fumaroli; and *Anne of the Island*, by L. M. Montgomery.

In Chapter Five: *The Celebrated Jumping Frog of Calaveras County*, by Mark Twain; *Language, Thought, and Reality: The Selected Writings of Benjamin Lee Whorf*, edited by John B. Carroll; *The Language Instinct* and *The Stuff of Thought*, both by Steven Pinker; *What Language Is*, by John McWhorter; *Parlez-vous franglais?*, by Réné Etiemble; *Yoga for People Who Can't Be Bothered to Do It*, by Geoff Dyer; *Studies on Hysteria*, by Josef Breuer and Sigmund Freud; *The Language of Food*, by Dan Jurafsky; *Rules of the Wild*, by Francesca Marciano; and *Giovanni's Room*, by James Baldwin.

In Chapter Six: *Daughters of the King and Founders of a*

Nation: Les Filles du Roi in New France, a master's thesis by Aimie Kathleen Runyan; *Language in Canada*, by John Edwards; *The Fish People*, by Jean E. Jackson; and *Granite Island*, by Dorothy Carrington.

The insights of several books suffuse the entirety of the one I ended up writing. I'm indebted to *The Bilingual Mind*, Aneta Pavlenko's groundbreaking study of language and thought; Umberto Eco's dazzlingly synthetic *The Search for the Perfect Language*; and *The Story of French*, an indispensable history of the language, written by Jean-Benoît Nadeau and Julie Barlow, a Canadian couple (he, French-speaking; she, English-speaking) whose harmonious output gives the rest of us hope. Eva Hoffman's *Lost in Translation* is a beautiful memoir about exile, from home and language. Alice Kaplan's *French Lessons* is one of the most beautiful memoirs of them all.

I'm grateful to a number of experts who took the time to answer my very basic questions about very complicated subjects. I profited tremendously from the erudition and generosity of Arif Ahmed, Lisa Barrett, Guy Deutscher, Jean Jackson, Graham Jones, Dan Jurafsky, Richard Kieckhefer, Anthony Lodge, Peter Maslowski, and Aneta Pavlenko. Whatever mistakes or misunderstandings I am certain to have committed are mine alone. Liam McNulty at the London Library was kind enough to identify Hermes of Praxiteles and to double-check a quote. Katia Zorich translated the section of *Drugie berega* in which Nabokov describes his childhood home into English. Andy Young performed a masterful and possibly even enjoyable fact-check of the manuscript. Alice Mahoney cleaned up my many *fautes* in French.

Ann Godoff has been a dream editor: curious, decisive, crazy-responsive. Casey Rasch, her assistant, is exceptional.

I'm also beholden to Sarah Hutson, Juliana Kiyan, Matt Boyd, Caitlin O'Shaughnessy, and Will Heyward for all their work on my behalf.

I am lucky to have Elyse Cheney on my side. And she's lucky to have Sam Freilich, Alex Jacobs, and Adam Eaglin. Natasha Fairweather is outstanding in every way.

David Remnick: I may have to resort to box-set Italian to thank you for being the *capo di tutto capi*, and, beyond that, a real friend. I'm beyond privileged to work with Dorothy Wickenden, Daniel Zalewski, John Bennet, Susan Morrison, Nick Paumgarten, Ben McGrath, Lizzie Widdicombe, Mary Norris, Leo Carey, Betsy Morais, Emily Greenhouse, and Jiayang Fan, who have given me, in addition to help on this book, years of encouragement, counsel, and companionship. I'm also grateful to have had the opportunity, in my work at *The New Yorker*, to begin playing with some of the ideas that I've developed more fully here. In a few spots, I've used fragments—sometimes reworked, sometimes verbatim—of pieces I've written about language.

Ed Caesar read this book, in all its incarnations, as attentively as if it were one of his own. Lila Byock, my other secret weapon, is the friend I wanted all my life. Silvia Killingsworth, Charlotte Faircloth, Hadley Freeman, and Guillaume Gendron improved what I wrote as much as they do life in general. Helen Walsh, Spruill Hayes, Amy Campos, Amelia Boisseau, and Christina Chandler have been there for everything. The women of It's Friday transformed Geneva and I miss them.

The love and effort of Jhenny dela Rosa, Cherry Rodrigo, and Let Let Mallari have made it possible for me to work.

Violeta, Teddy, Jacques, Hugo, Fabrice, *et* Anne-Laure—*merci mille fois pour votre affection et votre soutien tout au long de ce projet; merci de m'avoir accueillie dès le début, cafetière comprise; merci d'être ma famille.* Matt and Melissa—I couldn't ask for better. Please come visit soon. Dad, those times with you made me who I am. Mom, you are extraordinary, my bedrock. I know it now more than ever. Olivier! I don't know if I said it all, but I tried. *C'est à tes côtés que je me suis épanouie. Je t'aime, et je l'aime, notre petite abeille.*